Proving Manhood

Men and Masculinity
Michael Kimmel, Editor

Proving Manhood

Reflections on Men and Sexism

Timothy Beneke

UNIVERSITY OF CALIFORNIA PRESS

BERKELEY LOS ANGELES LONDON

Excerpts from Theodore Roethke's "In a Dark Time" and "His Foreboding" reprinted by permission of Doubleday, Dell Publishing Group, Inc., from *The Far Field*, Theodore Roethke, 1964.

Excerpt from Emily Dickinson's poem #1123 reprinted by permission of the publishers and the Trustees of Amherst College from *The Poems of Emily Dickinson*, Thomas H. Johnson, ed., Cambridge, Mass.: The Belknap Press of Harvard University Press, © 1951, 1955, 1979, 1983 by the President and Fellows of Harvard College.

University of California Press
Berkeley and Los Angeles, California

University of California Press, Ltd.
London, England

© 1997 by
The Regents of the University of California

Library of Congress Cataloging-in-Publication Data

Beneke, Timothy.
    Proving manhood : reflections on men and sexism / Timothy Beneke.
        p.   cm.
    Includes bibliographical references and index
    ISBN 0-520-20961-3 (alk. paper)
    1. Men—United States—Psychology.   2. Masculinity (Psychology)—United States.   3. Men—United States—Sexual behavior.   4. Sexism—United States.
    5. Homophobia—United States.   I. Title.
    HQ1090.3.B45   1997
    305.31—dc21   97-1210
                                                                                    CIP

Printed in the United States of America
9   8   7   6   5   4   3   2   1

The paper used in this publication meets the minimum requirements of American National Standards for Information Sciences—Permanence of Paper for Printed Library Materials, ANSI z39.48-1984.

For Janice Heiss

Contents

Acknowledgments

Chuck Stephen has been a vital friend; it would be impossible to say what I have learned in our freewheeling conversations over the years—it has been a lot. Bob Blauner offered his acute perceptions of the manuscript; I treasure his wisdom. Michael Kimmel has provided a model of pro-feminist energy and intelligence for many years, and been a generous supporter of my work. Eli Sagan's 1986 seminar on psychoanalytic social theory in the Berkeley Sociology Department provided the seeds for many of the theoretical ideas in this book. Gabe Gesmer taught me a great deal about the unconscious and about how to listen, to myself and others. Phillip Tetlock's wonderfully lucid lectures on social psychology had a profound influence on my thinking.

Alan Acacia has been a generous benefactor and friend of this book, and an inspiring antisexist man. He, along with two other men, once leapt onto the stage of the Miss California Pageant when the winner was announced and shouted out, "Men resist sexism!"

Barbara Dixson was a kind and generous long-distance friend, and a balm to my soul.

I also want to thank Tim Nonn, Jim Stockinger, Kathy Anolick, Josh Gamson, Richard Isay, Josh Koestenbaum, Allan Creighton, Tom Tyler, Ben Orlove, and Judith Newton.

I want to thank Naomi Schneider of the University of California Press, both for her perceptive comments on the manuscript and her strong support of the project. Wendy Belcher's astute and challenging copyediting significantly improved the manuscript.

I want to thank my agent, Rhoda Weyr, for her professionalism.

And finally, most of all, I want to thank Janice Heiss, to whom this book is dedicated. Without her kindness and wit and joy, it might never have been written.

Preface

This book simultaneously explores men's sexism and men's pain, and is thus in danger of justifying, or, at the very least, appearing to justify, sexism. I want to address this danger from the outset by placing the book in an autobiographical context.

Starting in 1980, I was a part of a group of men who actively spoke out against sexism, trying to "get men to take responsibility for violence against women." We were struck by the fact that a terrible problem existed in violence against women, and that men—those collectively responsible—had yet to seriously acknowledge the problem, much less *do* anything about it. We would appear before a group of students, solemnly quote disturbing statistics, echo feminist anger, offer critiques of the social construction of male sexuality, identify continuities between "normal" male sexuality and rape, point out what beasts men were, and argue that it all had to change. Feminist women would thank us for "doing this work"——and men would give us a lot of blank stares. Though we would have claimed otherwise, we were really talking to the women present; we were reflecting our own alienation from men and our hatred of ourselves as men; and, at first, we were probably doing very little good. It soon became apparent: the road we were traveling led nowhere.

Over the years, antisexist men have attempted to evolve a strategy that would enable them to be heard by other men. As the late Harrison Simms of the Oakland Men's Project put it: "I'm convinced that a man can't listen to a woman tell him about what sexism has done to her when he can't even acknowledge what's happened to him as a man. The first thing for men to notice—and we can't do it alone—is what a catastrophe sexism and masculinity are for us. Men are dying to notice this. My experience is that if you give men an atmosphere in which they feel safe to talk about that which 99 percent of the time it is *not* safe to talk about, all their pain about what was done in the name of making them men comes pouring out. Men aren't going to stop sexism for women, but I'm convinced they'll do it when they see what a disaster it is for them."[1]

I start from a recognition that men have enormous work to do to end sexism and that men's writing about sexism should serve that end. But I also recognize that men are not likely to venture forth as moral soldiers striving to end sexism unless they perceive it to be in their simple self-interest.

I am not confident about the likelihood of large numbers of men confronting sexism in an organized way any time soon. But I do think that a number of salient forces are at work in American (and other) societies to diminish the oppression of women. Those forces are:

Women gaining a measure of economic independence.

Women and men working side by side in the workplace seeking to solve problems together.

Men's increasing contribution to childrearing, especially in early childhood.

Women's increased economic power will continue to force men to take sexism more seriously. As I read the evidence of social psychology, men and women competently working together to achieve goals in the workplace should encourage men to see women as equals. And as fathers raise young boys, offering a nurturant model of identification— and as boys no longer find themselves making wrenching shifts in identification from their mothers to their fathers to become men—masculinity will be less psychically problematic for boys and men, who will have less need to denigrate women to prove they are men.

Only the last point is investigated in this book, which explores the subjectivity of manhood as it relates to sexism. It is written as part of a larger project of pro-feminist men to decenter masculinity, to make masculinity more visible as another phenomenon in the world, and not just the invisible patriarchal light by which reality is seen.

The philosopher Richard Wollheim observes that when we interpret others we begin with intuition; when we interpret ourselves we start from introspection.[2] This book leans heavily on both. I am not formally trained in any advanced academic discipline; I am not a therapist calling upon clinical experience, or a social scientist drawing upon methodically derived and assessed evidence. I do have substantial experience as an antisexist activist, and I spent considerable time in the early 1980s interviewing men on the subject of rape. My methods are simply to draw on those intellectual tools that are within my grasp. My background is white, middle-class, and heterosexual. Unless otherwise stated, when I refer to men in this book I am focusing on straight, white, American men, though it is my hope and belief that what I have to say will apply, with appropriate emendations, to other men as well.

I have little to say in this book about the plurality of masculinities that exists in American culture. I identify ideal types of masculine behavior and experience that I hope adequately describe enough men to shed light on sexism. This book is more diagnostic than prescriptive; I have tried to explore what is rather than suggest what should be. I find it impossible to write without hearing worthy voices in the wings warning of the dangers of ethnocentrism and essentialism, but I have let the voices remain silent to avoid being mired in circumlocution. I recognize that there are many masculinities—informed by, among other things, subculture, class, race, ethnicity, age, disability, and personal idiosyncrasy—which I have not specifically addressed. And there are, no doubt, more sexisms as well. But there are also buried commonalties in men that can be excavated and given light. It is these upon which I have focused.

Introduction

In an earlier work, *Men on Rape,* I explored the psychological pain that lay beneath certain men's justification of rape;
but I largely dismissed this pain as deluded or illusory
because of the outrageous purposes to which it was put.
I would interview men and hear them—often speaking
through a fog of bewilderment and confusion—offer egregious justifications of rape. While appalled at what they said,
I felt a guilt-ridden empathy and sadness that I struggled to
repress. How could I feel such empathy for these overtly sexist men? How could I so easily identify with their pain? In
describing them to women, or speaking about them in public, I would quickly distance myself from these men and dismiss, or even ridicule, their distress, just as I would down-
play any acknowledgment of men's distress in general. I did
this, consciously and unconsciously, for a variety of reasons
and motives: fear of justifying, or appearing to justify, sexism by empathizing with sexist men; fear of awakening in

myself "politically incorrect" feelings or being ensnared in sexist world views; diffuse guilt over my privilege as a white man; fear of appearing to solicit sympathy and nurturance from women; and fear of women's disapproval. I was also unconsciously influenced by the dominant tradition of men opposing violence against women that exists in American history—one by which men adopt a "pure" heroic self-image and view women as helpless, "pure" victims.

I think my dismissal of men's pain, although at the time arguably prudent and politic (and personally safe), is now both politically and intellectually misguided. Men who support feminism, and attempt to confront sexism in their own lives, are the only participants in the ongoing conversation on gender who both acknowledge the problem of sexism and possess a firsthand grasp of its sources in men's experience.

There exists a set of writings by men that points to the difficulties of being a man and a set of writings that address sexism. But the two do not sufficiently engage each other. The pains of manhood pointed to by anti-feminist men or mythopoeticists are, for the most part, not *merely* a matter of self-pity, indulgence, or the rationalization of sexism, although they can often serve such ends. I am trying in this book to distinguish distress in men from the *uses* that are made of distress; this is a necessary distinction if we are to understand the sources of sexism and seek to end it.

•   •   •   •   •   •

This book makes use of different styles and approaches. I am, by turns, autobiographical, psychoanalytic, sociological, phenomenological, and political. My concerns are of a piece, however. I have tried to use those tools at my disposal to constructively advance an understanding of men and sexism. I write in three voices intended to complement and echo each other: a personal voice in which I reflect on my experience as a man; a more theoretical voice engaged in the exposition and application of ideas; and a political voice committed to ending sexism and violence against women. The theoretical voice aims to illumine the meaning of personal experience, while the personal voice aims to give flesh to what can seem like abstract theorizing; the political voice informs and guides the book's soul and spirit. In recent years much of the important theorizing about men has been done by women, who, by definition, lack firsthand access to men's experience. Drawing heavily upon psychoanalytic feminist theory, I attempt to deepen and clarify the relation between theory and male experience in what follows.

The theoretical reflections in this book tend to revolve around the issues of identification and disidentification and their attendant perils and confusions: the tenuous and troublesome shift in identification of boys from their mothers to their fathers in early childhood; the way adolescent boys are traumatized into identification as men in some cultures; the way having sex sometimes threatens straight men with identification with women and thus becomes defensively dominative; the way homoerotic fantasy in straight men can be motivated by identification with women; and the way gay men may be motivated toward ambivalent identification with women, first through their attraction to their fathers as boys and then through what I call the Sexual Attraction Ratio.

In chapter 1, "Reflections of an Antirape Activist," I attempt to retrieve useful insights and perceptions from my experience as an antirape activist in the early 1980s. I think that, sooner or later, women will force men to take rape and violence against women seriously and to actively work to stop it but I have no idea when this will happen. Antirape work is confusing terrain for men, and those of us who have wandered in it need to retrieve whatever insight we can—or at least talk openly about our experience. I explore, among other things, the psychological processes and concrete experiences that led me to care passionately about the subject; the inevitable guilt that follows upon engagement with the topic; the emotions (repressed and otherwise) rooted in childhood experience that informed my anger at men and made possible my empathy for women; the confusion that followed from being perceived by women as "better" than I was; the evanescent quality of the insights achieved; and the enormous gulf that separates the sexes.

In chapter 2, "Proving Manhood," I look at compulsive masculinity: the compulsion to create and conquer stress and distress as a way of proving manhood and asserting men's superiority to women. I argue that pain—stress and distress of any kind—is problematic for men in ways that threaten manhood and lead to sexism. Everywhere in the United States, and in other cultures, we see boys and men taking distress "like a man" and feeling implicitly superior to women; this theme is alive and echoes powerfully even in the psyches of men who consciously oppose sexism. Virtually any stress or distress—physical pain, situations of danger, challenges, excessive consumption of alcohol, fear, "grossness," grief—can serve as occasions for boys and men to prove manhood. I argue that, while the objective stresses of a culture will influence compulsive masculinity, its sources are usefully explained through the application of ideas derived from psychoanalytic feminist Nancy Chodorow. Predominantly mother-raised boys come into life more or less identified with their mothers and must, at a certain point, make a wrenching shift to identify with their fathers. Thousands of times in the first two years of life, boys experience intense stress and distress in the form of hunger, physical pain or discomfort, and fear; they respond to this by seeking out the safety of identifying with and melding with mother. Identification with mother's safety becomes gradually unsafe as boys come to identify with a father who is often absent. Boys come to identify less with a person and more with a position, a status as male, through identifying with the grandiose stereotypes of masculinity that the culture offers.

But boys never quite pull it off; they are never quite sure they are men and tend to feel only as masculine as their last demonstration of masculinity. Their early childhood experience leaves them with what Freud calls an instinctual demand—a strong desire, or a set of strong desires—to regress and identify with mother when they experience distress, just as they did so often in early life. But to do so threatens them with the loss of their tenuously held sense of themselves as masculine. According to Freud, neurotic anxiety develops when we have a strong desire that is dangerous to experience because it threatens our sense of self (our ego or sense of "I-ness") and because of the responses we would get from others if we acted on it; so we develop symptoms and inhibitions that keep the desire at bay and offer substitute gratification. Boys have a strong desire to regress and identify with their mothers, or at least to return to a state prior to their awareness of gender where they safely melded with them; the experience of stress and distress evokes this desire. So they treat moments of stress and distress as occasions to prove masculinity by "taking it like a man."

I also draw on findings from social psychology that suggest that ingroup/outgroup prejudice is deeply rooted in our natures and that hits to our self-esteem cause us to engage in BIRGing—basking in reflected glory. I argue that distress tends to be experienced by boys and men as a threat to self-esteem in the form of a threat to manhood—the desire to regress and identify with mother that is awakened by distress threatens self-esteem. One way boys and men cope with this is to take flight into male glory, which can be seen as a substitute for infantile safety.

Chapter 3, "Pornography, Sexism, and Male Heterosexuality," looks at these topics from a variety of perspectives. I draw upon styles of thinking found in Erving Goffman's microsociology, psychoanalytic feminism, cognitive science, and social psychology. I focus first on boys' and men's social experience of seeing women and then distinguish among authorized, stolen, intrusive, and authorized/stolen images of women. I examine feelings of resentment in men attached to the experience of stolen and intrusive images, feelings that form a background context for the experience of looking at pornography. I go on to argue that the concept of objectification tends to blind us to the central role of the woman's putative subjectivity in pornographic images of women. I argue that pornography must be understood, in part, in terms of the situation of masturbation, which itself constitutes a hit to men's self-esteem, and thus calls for a kind of BIRGing that is supported by the flattering images of women in pornography.

I also call upon psychoanalytic feminist ideas developed in chapter 2 related to men's fear of identifying with women. I argue that the experience of being held and having sex with a woman threatens some men with maternal identification, and that sex must be defensively dominative.

I go on to suggest that two underlying models of sex (sex as relating and sex as pleasure) and two models of sexism (whore sexism and Madonna sexism) have tended to govern political debates on pornography. I attempt to identify positions that follow from each model. I close with a brief query into the relations between sexism and sexual repression.

In chapter 4, "Reflections on Mothers, Grief, and Sexism," I return to a personal voice and look at my relationship to my own mother in an attempt to connect my experience of her with the theorizing about men and their mothers that appears in the previous two chapters. I explore my grief over my mother's death when I was thirteen; the importance of giving up the overidealized myth of motherhood; the relation between men's grief and the capacity to empathize with women; my learning to swear as a mode of separation from my mother; experiences of "disempowering" my mother through proving manhood; and my awareness of a longing to meld with her.

Chapter 5, "The Sports Page," takes off from one morning's real-time experience of the sports page to explore the manhood-proving side of sports. I look at the way I garner self-esteem through vicarious identification with sports figures; the death metaphors of baseball and their relation to manhood proving; my guilt over the pleasure I take in the sports page; how my BIRGing in sports figures embarrasses me because it clashes with intellectual grandiosity; how sports filled a hole in my identity as I sought to prove manhood as a child; and the mystery and magic of baseball statistics and the hold they still have over my mind and mood.

In chapter 6, "Homophobia," I start from a contradiction best expressed by Jeffrey Weeks: male heterosexuality is presented as the most natural thing in the world, and yet so many straight men behave as if it were perpetually fragile, and in danger of being undercut or destroyed by any contamination with gays. The fragility of something so supposedly natural can be understood in terms of the equation of heterosexuality with masculinity. The uncoupling of the two would strike a blow against both homophobia and sexism—if heterosexual desire and activity did not prove masculinity, homosexual desire and activity would not disprove it.

I examine some psychoanalytic sources of homophobia. I start from the assumption that homosexuality is genetically driven and argue that fantasies of sexual acts may not express sexual desire. I distinguish among lust toward one's own sex that is driven toward orgasm; an affectional consciousness toward one's own sex; and fantasies of sexual activity toward one's own sex that are not charged with lust. I go on to look at three developmental moments. First, in the preoedipal identification of boys with their mothers, the boy sees the world and his father through his mother's eyes, and possesses an acquired erotic perception of his father. Second, when the boy transfers identification to his father he also transfers attraction. Third, as the boy grows up, the mother presents a vision of men for him to identify with; he is encouraged to identify with her eroticized image of what is a good man. All three of these moments are potential sources of homophobia.

I call upon gay psychoanalyst Richard Isay's observation that homoerotic fantasies in straight men often express unconscious desires to be like women. I end with a look at the ways straight men injure themselves in trying to demonstrate that they are not gay.

In chapter 7, "Gay Sexism," I identify three forms of sexism that are distinctive to gay men: a certain willful, perhaps tacitly hostile, ignoring of straight women; a certain appropriation and mocking of, and competitiveness toward, the "feminine" and women's heteroerotic attractiveness; and a certain denigration of the "feminine" as it is found in gay men. I then look at what is structurally common to gay men's experience that might lead to the sexism I described. I identify four structures as possible sources. First, gay men are not attracted to women and do not form primary economic and affectional bonds with them (a structure that also works *against* gay men's sexism). Second, straight women can be homophobic. Third, gay men are attracted to their fathers at a young age and are in competition with their mothers and with women (here I draw upon Richard Isay's work). Finally, what I call the Sexual Attraction Ratio (SAR) is at work to increase gay sexism. That is, 90+ percent of those people that gay men are attracted to (men) are not attracted to them (because they are heterosexual), and 90+ percent of those who are attracted to them (women), gay men are not attracted to. While acknowledging the limitations of these categories, I argue that, especially in a closeted world, the SAR will have profound psychic implications for gay men that encourage sexism.

In the epilogue I more explicitly explore some connections between sexism and the pains of manhood: the various ways sexism is a pain for men and the pains of manhood drive men into sexism. I draw upon activist Allan Creighton to suggest one poignant approach to men's sexism, and close by expressing my own weariness with masculinity, and identity itself.

Finally I offer an appendix, "Thinking About Sexism," in which I try to conceptually unpack the notion of sexism and show its complexity. I offer it as a corrective against the tendency to view sexism as one thing, one essence, that we can use as a tool to inspect reality. Many things may be going on, or not going on, when sexism occurs. I suggest that sexism breaks down in ways that are worth making explicit. I offer thirteen distinctions within sexism itself, and one between sexism and gender oppression generally.

1

Reflections of an Antirape Activist

What's madness but nobility of soul
At odds with circumstance?
Theodore Roethke

I spent much of 1980 and part of 1981 reading, talking, thinking about, and above all interviewing men about, rape. I was writing a book and speaking out, trying to be of use to the world. I interviewed men of as many stripes as possible: men who defended rapists and men who prosecuted them; men who treated rape victims; men who admitted to rape and men who committed acts others would call rape; men who were turned on by rape fantasies and men who could never find such fantasies erotic; men who tracked down rapists; men whose wives and girlfriends had been raped; men on the street; good men, bad men, sexist men, and antisexist men.

And I was experimenting with my consciousness. I tried to identify with the most abused rape victims, the worst rapists, and everyone in between; I wanted, through writing and speaking, to exert just the right influence that would stimulate the right kind of social change—social change that would help end violence against women. My view of myself was heroic and at times grandiose; my mood was sometimes manic. At times I felt like a fraud, strangely distant from my social identity. I tended to move between a heartfelt earnestness mingled with false piety on the one hand, and an awkward, guilty irony that covered disquieting feelings on the other. Earnestness can be exhausting. I was trying to be the good boy my mother wanted me to be; I was full of repressed anger at my father that made it easier to feel angry at men; and I was working off guilt that had little to do with anything I had actually done. I generally had enough sanity and objectivity to try to put my ego and conflicts aside and to direct my energies where they might be of use.

I was often viewed by women as someone I wasn't. I pretended to feel more than I actually felt; I felt much that I believed I was supposed to feel and pretended not to feel much that I did. I sometimes half knew when I was pretending, sometimes truly knew, and often didn't know at all. In presenting a persona to women that denied my feelings and fantasies, I sometimes got lost. Certain of my selves were not speaking to each other—or even acknowledging each other. It is sometimes claimed that activists are as concerned with upholding images of themselves as progressives as they are with effecting change. I suffered a bit from this malady.

I tried to identify with rape and found it disturbingly easy. I felt murky guilt about this. For a time I saw male sexuality as almost evil. I had days when I felt identified with lesbian separatism and days when I got sick of the arrogance of radical feminists who claimed knowledge about men they didn't possess.

Burdened (or is it lightened?) with a hapless sense of life's absurdity, I still felt all this was something wonderfully worth doing.

I want to go back, to look at this period, to see what of value can be retrieved, to explore. Who and what I was back then both embarrasses me and gives me pride. Or maybe, what I *was* embarrasses; what I *did* I am proud of and lives on a little. I am not here interested in therapeutic exploration for its own sake, though this process is therapeutic. My best motive is to shine a light on certain aspects of my consciousness in a way others may find useful.

My job was to understand and explain men to women, and to "get men to take responsibility for violence against women" (the words feel so leaden and overfamiliar I can barely write them). I still take it as obvious that we have a terrible problem in men: men's violence toward women; toward other men; toward themselves. And I take it as obvious that few men are able to acknowledge the problem, much less do something about it. That recognition guides and informs everything I write about men, no less so here.

· · · · ·

It is early August 1979, 9:30 at night. Nancy, with whom I have recently become involved, is waiting for a bus across from a Berkeley fraternity house. At twenty-one, she is petite, blond, and possessed of an openness toward the world that fascinates me. Across the street fraternity men are sitting on the porch, boisterously drinking beer. For a couple of minutes, they shout:

"Hey pussy hair!"

"Hey sweetie!"

"Hey baby, wanta drink some beer?"

Drunken, boorish laughter punctuates their shouts.

Nancy soon begins to tremble, scared. One of the men ambles up to her and says, "Hey, I made a bet with my buddies! Are you standing there 'cause you're waiting to be raped?"

Nancy is terrified. She summons her courage and blurts out with as much force as she can muster, "I think you're really *sick!*"

"Hey fellows, she thinks I'm really *sick!*"

The fraternity men laugh. The man returns to his buddies to continue their revelry. The suffering they are causing gives them pleasure.

Nancy continues to tremble and fights back tears. She does not understand why they are doing this. Soon the bus comes and saves her from these goons.

She waits until the next day to tell me what happened. While she recounts the incident I feel an intense rage at these men—it is the first time I feel this much rage over the things men do to women. While I know many women who have been abused by men, I somehow never felt very angry about it. Nancy feels helpless, resigned, depressed. She asks a question I will hear many times in the next couple of years, "*Why* are they *so* angry?"

I have many answers for her, all inadequate. The question reverberates inside me. I encourage her to take action. If she can reclaim some power she will feel less victimized and dispirited by the experience, and, anyway, the fraternity men should not be allowed to get away with it. She decides to write a letter of protest to the fraternity, the Interfraternity Council, and the student newspaper. The next day, along with another male friend, we go to the fraternity house and ask to speak to the head of the fraternity. Although scared, Nancy describes what happened the previous night and informs them that they will be receiving a letter of protest. There is a mood of polite, tense embarrassment in the fraternity.

She publishes the letter in the student paper—it is welcomed in the community. It turns out that the members of this fraternity have caused other people problems and have a bad reputation. They are put on probation by the university. One false move and they will be forced to shut down.

Nancy feels, momentarily at least, empowered.

Several weeks later. I have spent the summer working as a fund-raiser and community organizer for a Berkeley environmental group. One of the women I work with, Sheila, is from Trinidad and has been in the United States for little over a year. In addition to being astute and fun loving, she is generally regarded as beautiful. Sheila at times speaks of the cowardly way American women live their lives and resolutely refuses to curtail her freedom.

Several coworkers have gotten together for a party at

Sheila's house. A strong feeling of community exists among us. Sheila is going camping in the wilderness with a friend who will be heading back east. Sheila will be finding her way back alone and plans to hitchhike.

As the evening comes to a close and we part, I say to a friend: "I wonder what America's going to do to Sheila." I do not consciously think of rape.

I am not speaking from any well-informed feminist consciousness. I want to see myself and be seen by women as an estimable person, but my grasp of feminist ideas is superficial. It has simply become a part of my background picture of the world that women are brutalized in America, and that any woman who assumes the freedoms Sheila assumes is vulnerable.

A week later I hear that Sheila was raped at gunpoint by a trucker who picked her up hitchhiking. She knew the name of the trucking firm and where the truck was located when she was picked up, and she reported it to the police. It would have been easy for the police to examine the company's records and determine who was driving the truck, but they chose not to.

As she left the police station the officer said, "I don't want to be crude or nothin', but your rapist sure knows how to pick 'em."

I feel horrified, but keep the incident at a psychic distance.

A couple of months later I am reading Susan Brownmiller's *Against Our Will.*[1] Brownmiller remarks how little Freud and Jung have written about rape. This strikes me as curious; the idea occurs to me to do a book exploring men's attitudes toward rape. For a couple of years I have vaguely defined myself as wanting to write books. I begin interviewing men in a loose, open-ended way. I start educating myself. I reflect upon the women I have known and can readily count six who have been raped, as well as several others upon whom it has been attempted. I review my adolescent aggressiveness toward women and can easily find incidents in which I used my anger, and implicitly, my superior physical strength, to get sex. Nothing that most people would call rape, but, at the least, extracting ambivalent consent under psychological duress.

Nancy and I start living together. For whatever reason—because she is blond, little, open, "cute"—she is harassed more than most women. Men shout things at her or come on to her. She rides a bicycle and is harassed by men in cars. I see, or think I see, something being damaged in her, a certain wonder and openness that I cherish, and I am further outraged. I am twenty-nine; she is twenty-one. I am fatherly and avuncular toward her. I cherish her sensitivity and try to nourish her talents. She is a talented artist, a musician, a poet, a shrewd political organizer committed to social justice. I am charmed by her; I take refuge in an identity as the knowing father. It protects me from my own fears and confusion. I find that she is living daily with a certain fear that I can easily identify with.

I am also afraid of men. When I was ten my father beat up my mother, ran everyone out of the house, and broke most of the furniture. It is by far the most powerful memory of my childhood. For the next couple of years he was often on the edge of violence. I never again felt safe around him and lived with the unthinkable fear that he would kill us all. With my father ranting outside my door, I spent many nights with a pillow over my head and butterflies in my stomach, praying I would fall asleep and wake up the next morning with him gone to work. (He was a colonel in the army.) I organized my time to avoid him. When I was around him, I constantly assessed his mood. At times he was better, at times worse; there was much about him that was good and that I loved, but I was never again unafraid of him.

And I did not feel anger toward him until I was thirty-nine, five years after his death, a decade after the incident with Nancy, and nine years after I began speaking out against men's violence toward women.

And in the strange way such things are possible, I both did and did not know that my father had beaten up my mother that night. I knew, in the sense that I saw the bruises on her the next day and remembered her lying with ice packs against her discolored jaw. But I also did *not* know in that I never actually admitted to myself that he had beaten her up. I'm not sure what or how or *if* I thought about it. I was in a state of prolonged psychic numbness—my thought processes had frozen in a kind of denial at age ten. Perhaps it was too painful to admit what had happened even though I *knew* what had happened—all the information was alive in my conscious memory.

So it was easy for me to identify with Nancy's fear of violent men and to feel angry at them. I carried a lot of free-floating fear and organized my life as best I could (not very well) to avoid the competitive world of men. I lived cheaply, worked at part-time jobs on the fringes, and would have been called a Berkeley hippie.

It was, above all, my ability to empathize with Nancy's (and women's) fear, and to feel outraged at the cause of it, that fueled my outrage against violence against women.

·   ·   ·   ·   ·

Six months after beginning my book in 1980, I am wanted on the local media. There is a need for "sensitive new men" who can talk about rape. I feel somewhat fraudulent in the role. There is little in my past to recommend me for it. I spent a year in graduate school on a fellowship, successfully posing as a clever philosophy student; I have read eclectically and loosely in several areas but still have not read much feminism. I am not a sociologist or psychologist or a trained interviewer. But I am appalled by the enormity of the problem of rape and violence against women and men's silence on the issue. Obviously, men must do a huge amount of work before meaningful changes will occur. *Someone* needs to say what I am saying and do what I am doing. I am embraced by a small community of women and men in the San Francisco

Bay Area who have worked and thought seriously about all this. They like what I am doing and connect me to their network.

My first television appearance is on a Sunday morning show that has devoted the hour to rape. I appear with a woman from a rape crisis center, a prominent feminist folk singer, and a woman who teaches self-defense. My role is to explain men and serve as a model of the new man of the 1980s.

I feel unreal. How did I get myself in the position of explaining men to women? What am I doing here full of thoughts about rape? And what do I really know anyway? I have plenty of raps at my disposal but lack confidence in them.

I have not been on television since I was a child in the peanut gallery on the cartoon shows. As a man writing and speaking about rape, I possess a growing awareness of the legitimate suspicion that I invite. Some women on the show will judge me as guilty until I prove myself innocent. Probably a few women who feel so intensely identified with their anger at men on some level will *want* me to be insensitive and sexist. I may even disappoint them if I am decent and enlightened. They may even be unable to experience me as such. A number of women in the antirape movement have welcomed me warmly. I try to think of rape victims before I speak—I feel most answerable to them and the thought of them pulls me out of my self-involvement, which I recognize is a relatively trivial matter in the scheme of things.

I am sitting outside the studio trying to figure out what to say. I have been prepped by Rich Snowden and Allan Creighton, two activist friends whom I regard as better equipped to go on the show. But the show wants me. My intention is to use the interviewer's questions as jumping-off points to say what I want to say. I am prepared to be hard on men, in part because I am angry and in part because it is safe. The women whose approval I seek will find it difficult to fault my anger. My main task is to claim rape as a man's problem and to serve as a model that men can identify with. I feel resolute, ready to stir things up.

Inside, I am met by the host of the show, a heavyset woman whose eyes peer out from behind a shifting mountain of makeup. After introducing herself she says, "We're going to try to make this an 'up' show about rape, and we're not here to put down men."

My face contracts into a nutshell of civility. I nod in sheepish disorientation.

After escorting me into the studio, the host explains how we will proceed. "After we've taped the first two segments, we'll show an excerpt of an educational video showing teenagers on a date. We'll see a teenage boy taking his date home after spending a lot of money on her. She invites him inside; after a few minutes she decides to go to sleep and asks him to leave. He flies into a rage, insisting that she owes him sex, and violently forces himself on her. At that point the camera will focus on your face, and I'll ask your reaction to what we've just seen. Okay?"

"Okay."

Oh shit, I think. My first televised appearance and the camera will focus directly on my face as I respond to a rape. I am expected to display sensitivity and outrage in this wholly artificial setting. I had better show the right emotion. I sit anxiously on the side while the first segments are taped. I am overcome with the strangeness of sitting in a studio waiting my turn to go on. I am called up. I sit down and am set up for sound. A burly cameraman barks at me without a trace of irony, "Relax, man."

I am rapidly combing through things I want to say. Then the light goes on and we watch the video on a small monitor ten feet away. Two black teenagers on a date. It unfolds as the host has suggested. Just as the boy climbs on top and begins to strike the girl, she screams and the tape ends.

"With us in the studio today is Timothy Beneke, who is writing a book about men and rape. Tim, give us your reaction to what we just saw."

I opt for the safest response.

"Well, I found it pretty scary. The idea that someone would not only be able to, but *want* to have sex with someone else while brutalizing them, is disturbing. It reveals an inability on the part of the man to identify with fear. It's part of a larger problem in men of being unable to acknowledge painful emotions. I think you can only have sex with someone who is terrified if you are unable to experience your own terror. So I would place it in a larger context."

I have glommed on to a readily available insight that I am

not sure I even believe—but it sounds good. The show goes on. I make predictably sensitive comments about men and rape. I talk about the denial that exists throughout our culture and the need for men to come to terms with rape. I am scrambling to come up with insightful-sounding observations, whether I really believe them or not. I don't really know what I believe but it is too frightening to admit this to myself. The only thing I am really certain of is the enormity of the problem of rape and the relative silence of men.

A couple of days after the show is aired, a new friend who runs the Rape Prevention Education Program on the Berkeley campus calls me up and says I was the best thing on the show. She says she is proud to know me. It feels great. Another man active in men's issues tells me I should not wear suede shoes on television. They're too soft, will turn men off, and make me seem less of an authority. I am appalled.

•　•　•　•　•

After spending several months interviewing men, the clearest theme I uncover is a vengefulness toward women's capacity to arouse, a feeling that leads men to justify rape. I am familiar with this vengefulness because I felt it as an adolescent, not as something to justify rape but as part of my sexuality. It is a feeling that grows distant as I get older but that is still real to me. I felt tormented by the attractiveness of women during adolescence, and when I was sexually active in college, I would engage in sex not for pleasure, or even ego, but as a corrective to the painful longing I felt. When I discuss this vengefulness in men with women, they generally assume it must be alien to me. After all, I appear sensitive, thoughtful, and enlightened about feminist issues. (One woman playfully introduces me to another as a "man you can trust.") I represent the sexist justifications of rape that I hear from men as something I can report on and make sense of, but I don't let on how easy it is to identify with the feelings that underlie these justifications.

It soon became apparent that even brilliant women who had thought hard about rape had little grasp of certain key feelings in men. I remember meeting separately with two women who were well versed on the subject. One, a Ph.D. in political science from Stanford, had written a dissertation on rape laws and was now a professor at San Francisco State University. The other had a Ph.D. in linguistics, was highly regarded as a psycholinguist, and had published a psycholinguistic analysis of rape manuals used by the police. Both of them discussed my interviews with me—it had never occurred to them that men felt this way.

"I always think of men as having so much power that it never occurred to me that they could experience women's attractiveness as so powerful," said the linguist.

I am aware more than ever of the enormous gulf that divides the sexes. These two women hadn't a clue about something fairly basic to male psychology, something that most straight men could understand quickly.

· · · · ·

I wanted to understand how the threat of rape affected women's lives and spent time imagining how my life would be different if I were a woman. Walking at night, I would attempt to imagine how the world would look and feel if I were a woman. I asked women about the constraint the threat of rape placed on their lives. I was moved and outraged by what I heard . One woman described running the four blocks home from her bus stop at night; another walked clutching her car keys as a weapon. Yet another described making herself small and inconspicuous on the bus.

I realized that the threat of rape constituted a kind of assault on the meaning of the world: an assault that many women took for granted and seldom articulated, and that most men never noticed. The threat of rape altered the meaning and feel of night and nature; required women to have more money than men out of a need for safer housing and transportation; inhibited women's expressiveness; reduced the possibility of solitude; made women more dependent on men; and inhibited the freedom of the eye. In retrospect, what is most striking is how elusive such insights are, how quickly they fall away from my lived comprehension of women.

Women have written a lot about their difficulties reconciling their sexuality with their politics. Something similar holds true for pro-feminist men. My "job" was a strange one. I needed to psychically grasp everything men had to say to me about rape, no matter how egregiously sexist, while relating to the problem of violence against women with as much moral seriousness as possible. I found it easy to eroticize rape and nearly impossible to talk about this with women. I never had rape fantasies that I generated on my own, but I could "enjoy" reading about it under certain circumstances where it was framed as fantasy. This is true of many men and important to note because guilt over one's erotic connection to rape fantasies may disable men from creatively, or at least nondefensively, addressing the subject. Once in a group of fifteen actively pro-feminist men someone asked how many had gotten sexual pleasure out of fantasizing about rape—twelve raised their hands. We are still haunted by a Judeo-Christian tradition that morally equates thoughts with deeds; I agree that some thoughts are misguided and injurious to the self, but none inherently hurt other people.

A distinction is in order. It is no secret that rape fantasies are fairly common in the erotic repertoires of both men and women. And it is readily understood by progressive people that just because women can be turned on by fantasies of rape does not mean that women *want* to be raped. But the converse is not always so well understood. Being turned on by fantasies of rape need not mean that men, all things taken into account, *want* to rape. It no doubt means that men find something about the fantasy of rape psychically gratifying; for instance, it may satisfy anger or feelings of frustration or revenge. But what we find gratifying in fantasy we may find horrifying in reality. Being turned on by a fantasy of rape is not the same thing as having a desire to rape. Being turned on by a rape fantasy means that one is turned on by a rape fantasy, nothing more, nothing less.

In ways I dimly understand, trying to find rape in myself was bad for my sexuality. I went too far in assuming that anything that was aggressive or angry or degrading of women in my fantasy life or in my sexual feelings was bad. I failed to see that intercourse, fucking, making love, whatever it's called, may often, and sometimes simultaneously, contain both hostility and love; that the aggression in sex could be part of its power and thrill. I wanted to decontaminate myself of anything that resembled rape and rape values and anything that smacked of the objectification of women. This was naive and ultimately destructive.

I came to see that I could only feel certain emotions by using language that fueled the connection between sex and violence. For a time, I naively believed that language that implicitly legitimated the connection between sex and violence should be avoided, or spoken only in knowing irony. The most obvious example was "Fuck you!"—a rape sentiment if ever there was one. I was on the lookout for rape language and saw it everywhere. It did not take long to see that I could not feel my emotions if I could not spontaneously use certain phrases. If I couldn't say "Fuck!" or tell someone to "Fuck off" I couldn't feel angry. Every time I said, "Oh fuck!" or "Screw them," I would think to myself: "rape language." It was not sexist language exactly, but language that implicitly legitimated the connection between sex and aggression and degradation. I wound up concluding that it was impossible and probably fruitless to try to change this aspect of my language, much less a whole culture's language. Not only expressing but feeling emotion depends upon language. Take away the language and you take away the emotion.

I struggled with the word "bitch"—I intuitively felt it was inherently sexist but had trouble figuring out why. I sensed that it was a way of keeping women from being assertive and that it imposed a sexist model of femininity that demanded unreasonable nurturance and subservience from women. Except for one occasion when I felt deeply affronted by a woman, I have had no use for the word "bitch" in fourteen years. (I did not speak it to the woman, I only felt, and more important, *needed to feel,* she was a bitch.)

Because I was taking on sexist anger in men I found it hard to legitimate any anger a man might feel toward a woman, especially in relation to sex. After speaking publicly about rape maybe a hundred times, I could not bring myself to admit that a man might legitimately feel angry at a woman who was "teasing" him; I could not simply say that men have a right to express anger in a nonthreatening way to such a woman. Because I heard teasing used as a justification for rape, I unconsciously assumed it could never be a justification for anger, or that men could never express nonsexist anger at women over sex. I avoided letting myself think this because it was unsafe and, I thought, politically counterproductive to express. Certainly easily misunderstood.

•   •   •   •   •

Sixteen years after beginning this process, where does it leave me? I ended my book on men and rape with these words:

"How much longer will men accept as normal lives of constraint and abuse for women? I don't know. American men have an opportunity to reverse a part of history as old as history itself. History can happen fast. We must see that it happens soon."

There is yet little evidence that it will happen soon. The primary masculine tradition that opposes violence against women is a sexist one that arises out of fury after the fact of rape—"My woman was raped and I will kill whoever did it." In this tradition, women are viewed as property and only rape by strangers is "real" rape.

What strikes me now is how American masculinity has become a disenchanted symbol. The successful attempts to influence men have come from those like Robert Bly, and now the homophobic Christian Promise Keepers, who number nearly a million and explicitly seek to reassert masculine dominance. What Bly and the Promise Keepers have in common is their ability, in varying degrees misguided, to ennoble and reenchant masculinity—something men deeply yearn for.

Any attempt to get American men to take responsibility for rape and violence against women must find a way to ennoble and enchant manhood while retaining a sense of equality with women. *This* will not be easy.

•   •   •   •   •

Upon reading the above, a friend asked in frustration, "But *why* did you become pro-feminist?" I will try to answer, despite my self-distrust. I said that I had repressed anger at my father that made it easy to be angry at men. Some of this anger was over his violence toward my mother, some over the fear he caused me. At any rate I was not then in touch with the anger, though I knew there were objective reasons for its existence. I think the anger toward my father that I was repressing fed the anger I felt toward men.

And the fear I found in some women was accessible to me because of the fear I had known as a child. Women I was close to feared and were angry at men's violence; I could actively tap into my fear of my father's violence. What is most vivid in my motivations is the ease with which I could identify with women's fear of men.

When I asked the woman closest to me why I became a feminist, she said, only half in jest, "Because you want to be a *good* boy." In other words, because I want to please Mommy. Pleasing Mommy is part of the answer. It follows a certain logic: I see the women I know as I saw my mother; the women I know are all feminists; I want to please them so I became a feminist.

Also, I had a liberal consciousness formed in my adolescence in the early 1960s and a more radical one formed in the late 1960s. I lived in Berkeley for seven years in the 1970s. Berkeley was and is a place highly politicized and therapized—one of the few places where critiques of masculinity have been commonplace for twenty-five years.

Finally, I wanted to be a writer, but not just another writer with an ego, so I found a topic that needed air and light and made life a little less absurd. I was in the grip of some authentic political perception; I wanted to lend my voice to a cause I believed in.

All these things were at work in me.

2

Proving Manhood

Instead of coming to ourselves . . .
we grow all manner of deformities
and enormities.

Saul Bellow

Psychoanalytic feminist Nancy Chodorow makes a tantaliz-
ing statement: "Men have the means to institutionalize their
unconscious defenses against repressed yet strongly experienced developmental conflicts." [1]

What one wants is the details. Which institutions?
Through which psychic mechanisms and pathways are
"unconscious defenses against repressed yet strongly experienced developmental conflicts" institutionalized? And which
defenses and conflicts are central? How does it work? Chodorow also says: "Underlying, or built into, core male gender
identity is an early, nonverbal, unconscious, almost somatic
sense of primary oneness with the mother, an underlying
sense of femaleness that continually, usually unnoticeably,

but sometimes insistently, challenges and undermines the sense of maleness."[2]

In this chapter, I connect these two statements and the realities they address by showing that boys and men defend themselves against a desire to regress and identify with their mothers through institutionalizing a compulsion to prove their manhood, through creating and conquering stress and distress. I argue that psychic pain, whatever its source, is in and of itself problematic for men in ways that threaten men's identities as men, and leads men to prove manhood and assert superiority to women and to "failed" men—men who cope "poorly" with pain and gay men.

Why is it that successfully enduring distress is so central to proving manhood and proving superiority to women, not only in the United States, but in most of the cultures of the world? And why is it that manhood is something to be *proved*? And how do we confer manhood on men without also conferring upon them superiority to women? Or is the very business of conferring manhood inherently problematic? I want to add analytic and phenomenological depth, clarity, and precision to answers already given by Chodorow, Dorothy Dinnerstein, Jessica Benjamin, and others.[3]

I will draw heavily on the work of psychoanalytic feminism and Freud's later theory of neurotic anxiety, and will apply certain concepts from existentialism. Finally, I will recast these problem in terms of findings drawn from social psychology.

COMPULSIVE MASCULINITY

By compulsive masculinity I mean the compulsion or need to relate to, and at times create, stress or distress as a means of both proving manhood and conferring on boys and men superiority over women and other men. Failure to do so results in the social or private perception that one is less than a man. One must take distress "like a man" or run the risk of being perceived as feminine—a "sissy" or "mama's boy."

The content of the stress and distress can be usefully divided into three general categories:

1. That which would hurt anyone, e.g., physical pain, physical danger, large quantities of alcohol.
2. That which poses a psychological danger owing to the meaning it is given in relation to manhood, e.g., failing to win a sporting contest, losing physical strength and skill as one ages, and crying in public.
3. That which poses the greatest threat of all to manhood (a special case of category 2)—women. I address this more thoroughly in chapter 3. (The issue of homoerotic desire and homophobia is an equal threat to manhood—I address these in chapter 6.)

I will further divide compulsive masculinity into what I witness (and manifest) as an American man and what can be gleaned from other cultures through anthropological and other data. It is useful to keep in mind the distinction between activities performed as masculinity-proving in themselves (like many rites of passage), and activities like work where proving masculinity is not the primary goal, but rather a secondary gratification that influences how work is done.

Compulsive Masculinity in the United States

American culture is replete with examples of compulsive masculinity. Witness Norman Mailer writing about Muhammad Ali, who had recently lost an agonizing championship fight to Joe Frazier, in *Life* magazine in March of 1971: "For Ali had shown America what we all had hoped was secretly true. He was a man. He could endure moral and physical torture and he could stand." [4]

It wasn't enough that Ali had shown himself to be a great fighter; winning had been too easy for him. Ali had taken Frazier's punishment "like a man" and remained competent and whole: "he could stand." He did not give up or burst into tears or go soft. According to Mailer "we *all*" could only be sure he was a man if he suffered and endured. Otherwise he was too much of a woman and not a real man, or he was a boy and, implicitly, too soft and attached to his mother— too feminine. Mailer assumes that admirers of Ali tacitly subscribed to this manhood ideology and that readers of *Life* magazine already understood it. No explanation was required.

That one of America's most famous writers could write this about America's (then) most famous athlete in one of

America's most popular magazines suggests the pervasiveness of this ideology. It was, and largely still is, central to American culture.

Tom Wolfe wrote about the "right stuff" that was required of men to be test pilots and astronauts. What was this right stuff? It was the ability to repeatedly endure severe physical and psychological distress—high g's; intense, physically induced anxiety; and rapid heartbeats—while remaining cool, competent, and able to make snap, life-or-death decisions. And this right stuff—possessed only by the few—Wolfe says, is nothing other than masculinity itself.[5]

Sociologist Michael Kimmel offers many examples in his essay on the cult of masculinity in the United States.[6] The National Commission on the Causes and Prevention of Violence stated that "proving masculinity may require frequent rehearsals of toughness, the exploitation of women, and quick aggressive responses" (237). To "rehearse toughness" is to repeatedly prove one's ability to withstand stress as a preparation for greater stress. Kimmel quotes General Homer Lea, writing in 1898: "the greatest danger that a long period of profound peace offers to a nation is that of creating effeminate tendencies in young men" (241). Without war to "masculinize" men, they are in danger of becoming like women. And the Boy Scout Manual of 1914 states:

> The wilderness is gone, the Buckskin Man is gone, the painted Indian has hit the trail over the Great Divide, the hardships and privations of pioneer life which did so

> much to develop sterling manhood are now but a legend
> of history, and we must depend upon the Boy Scout
> movement to produce the MEN of the future. (243)

Again, without stress or distress through which men could test their manhood, they risk becoming women or remaining boys.

It seems that virtually anything men experience as stressful can serve as an occasion to prove manhood, so long as it is also something experienced as stressful by women. It would appear unlikely that American men could prove masculinity doing something women find easy to do. Although, with the advent of a "mythopoetic men's movement," where men take pride and may even compete in displaying their feelings, it is possible that the ability to cry in public, something women do more easily than men, may become a means of proving manhood.

American men take pride in handling alcohol like a man—getting sick or drunk, becoming incompetent, too easily can threaten one's manhood. Boys and even men feel superior to women and other men through their greater capacity to handle "grossness": unpleasant sounds and smells, insects and rodents, dirt, and so on.

The whole domain of male sports constitutes an occasion for proving manhood. The ability to withstand physical pain and intense psychological pressure, as Ali had done, and remain competent, is a central part of this. Moments of physical danger, like facing a fast-moving baseball when at bat or on the field, or evading tacklers while carrying a football, are similar occasions. The sheer psychological pressure exerted by the importance of winning or performing well enables one to prove manhood. (I explore this theme at greater length in chapter 5.)

Hypermasculine G. Gordon Liddy, of radio talk and Watergate fame, as a child toughened himself by placing his hand on a burning flame without flinching and eating a cooked rat.[7] And part of what makes some popular after-shave lotions like Old Spice manly is the stinging pain they cause when rubbed on the face.

What defines a sissy on the playground is regression in the face of stress: bursting into tears when hurt, growing soft and "choking" at a crucial moment in a sporting event, giving in to fear and refusing to accept dares or take risks.

Work is another realm where the ethos of the playground is often transferred and where competence has often been equated with masculinity. It is an open question to what extent the training one receives to become a doctor, lawyer, or other professional is motivated by compulsive masculinity—and to what extent the entrance of large numbers of women into the higher levels of these professions will change them.[8] Nor is it clear the degree to which proving manhood constitutes a source of creativity in work.

Clearly, the army claims to make a man out of its entrants.[9] A popular television commercial for the army presents a soldier about to parachute from a plane. We hear a voice-over of him writing to his father, telling him that he would have been proud of him today. The soldier remembers what his father told him: "Being a man means putting your fear aside and doing your job."

The degree to which work is motivated by ulterior, manhood-proving needs is an issue that demands exploration. And, as technology increasingly renders men's superior physical strength of less value, mastering technology itself increasingly becomes an important realm for proving manhood, as the popularity of the television sitcom, *Home Improvement,* ironically attests.

Another means of proving manhood requires resisting the impulse to "go soft" and empathize with or nurture those who are suffering or weaker—a skill strongly needed to remain cold-blooded when confronting suffering or horror. It would appear that at least some of the evils of the world, e.g., sexism, fascism, homophobia, and racism, are, in varying degrees, then, ways that men prove their manhood. Men engaging in a gang bang, committing political torture, bashing a gay man; white men deriding blacks and boys torturing a bug, are all in danger of being regarded as less manly by other men if they empathize with or try to help the rape or torture victim, the gay or black man, even the bug. They resist the impulse to empathize with victims in order to prove manhood. Though men aren't likely to explicitly regard these experiences as suffering "taken like a man," it is what's expected of them.

And, similarly, men mock and feel superior to women or men whose need to nurture is easily aroused at the sight of babies or cuddly animals. The capacity to experience other beings as "cute" is the capacity to have one's desire to nurture aroused. Many men find this threatening to their manhood. Men rather often, and women seldom, refer sarcastically to the actions of others as "cute." Typically, it is a way of saying that, in trying to be clever, another man has been incompetent; "cute" is, in this sense, a denigration of manhood. If a baseball pitcher throws an odd pitch or a basketball player shoots a wild and spectacular shot, they may be accused of "trying to be cute," that is, of not being a real man. "Getting cute" is perceived as the equivalent of seeking nurturance, being feminine, and is thus unacceptable.

Learning to swear is an interesting domain for proving manhood; saying what (supposedly) no "good" woman would say is a way of advertising one's toughness and separation from women; one learns to endure the implicit fear of one's parents, and maybe, God. A good swear is the opposite of a good cry; it hardens one in a self-image of toughness and attempts to inspire fear in one's real or imagined cohorts and adversaries.

Symbols of masculinity often contain and express a history of suffering successfully endured. Think of tattoos, sculpted muscles, and scars. Such symbols convey a willingness and capacity to suffer for a masculine identity, an achieved and visible toughness.

Threats to manhood need not be explicit, conscious, or labeled; they can be deeply internalized and can manifest themselves as shadowy anxiety, guilt, or defensiveness, among other things. Proving manhood need not be dramatic or overt, rather, typically, it becomes internalized and characterological. What makes the need to prove manhood compulsive is that it can never be satisfied; one is momentarily a man and then the doubts reassert themselves—you're only as masculine as your last demonstration of masculinity. Men internalize a draconian model of masculinity that is inherently masochistic.

Relating to stress together is a common way that men bond—the greater the stress the stronger the bond. The extraordinary connection men feel at war has often been observed.[10] Compulsive masculinity is inherently social, no matter how isolated the man or boy engaging in it.[11]

Women constitute the third major category of stress that threatens manhood. I will address this more fully in chapter 3. For now, three points.

First, the presence of women when a man is encountering masculinity-threatening stress compounds the stress. Part of proving manhood includes being perceived by women as a "real man."

Second, in the realm of sex, manhood is proved through one's capacity to find sexual partners and to remain potent with them. Sex is often dominative for men, and sexual problems are typically seen more as problems of failed manhood than as sexual problems.[12] In American culture we seldom explicitly regard sex as an occasion to take distress "like a man." But we do regard it as a proving ground for masculinity, either in terms of success at finding sexual partners or performance in sex.

Third, men's competition with women in the workplace is increasingly a threat to masculinity; competence at work has been a defining feature of male identity and men's superiority to women.

Compulsive Masculinity in Other Cultures

According to anthropologist David Gilmore's research, most cultures possess ideologies of manhood that require the successful endurance of distress, irrespective of degree of industrialization or mode of social organization. Gilmore gives some thirty examples of compulsive masculinity in the first few pages of his book, *Manhood in the Making*.[13]

We can roughly distinguish those cultures that possess a clearly defined set of rituals that guides young men into manhood from those cultures in which nonritualized compulsively masculine behaviors are expected of men. I will give examples of the latter first.

On Truk island in the South Pacific, where the sea is the primary source of sustenance, masculinity is seen as "chancy" and men are encouraged to maintain their manhood by taking dangerous risks and thinking "manly" thoughts. As a consequence, they go deep-sea fishing in tiny dugouts and spear fishing in shark-infested waters. If they are unwilling to do this, their fellows, male and female, ridicule them as effeminate and childlike. On land, Trukese youths get in fights, drink excessively, and prove their manhood through sexual conquests.

On the Greek isle of Kalymnos, the men live by commercial sponge fishing and are known to dive into deep waters without diving equipment; many get the bends and are crippled for life. Young divers who exercise caution are ridiculed as effeminate.

Throughout urban Latin America, men prove their manhood by cheerfully enduring challenges and insults. The cult of machismo honors the willingness to take dangerous risks as a manner of male honor.

In the deserts of western Egypt among the Bedouins, "real men" are said to be afraid of nothing.

In southern Spain, the Andalusian men are expected to demonstrate *hombria,* which literally means "manliness." Hombria requires the maintenance of a stoic and courageous demeanor in the face of danger.

A manhood ideology can be found in Albert Camus's "Reflections on the Guillotine." "As a writer, I have always loathed avoiding the issue; as a *man,* I believe that the repulsive aspects of our condition, if they are inevitable, must merely be *faced in silence*" (emphasis added).[14]

And in Hegel's *Philosophy of Right:* "Women are educated—who knows how?—as it were by breathing in ideas, by living rather than by acquiring knowledge. The *status of manhood,* on the other hand, is attained only by the *stress of thought* and much technical exertion" (emphasis added).[15]

Turning to the more explicitly ritualized manhood training reported in Gilmore's *Manhood in the Making,* East Afri-
can boys from some cattle-herding groups are taken from
their mothers at adolescence and subjected to bloody cir-
cumcision rites intended to transform them into men. They
must submit to the agony of the knife without flinching. If a
boy cries out, blinks an eye, or turns his head, he and his
progeny will be deeply shamed for life as unworthy of manhood. Boys are then thrust into a world of cattle rustling,
raiding, killing, and survival in the bush. Only after a long
apprenticeship, which establishes their toughness and competence, are they allowed to return to society and take wives.

In Ethiopia, the Amhara call manhood, *wand-nat,* a form
of masculinity that involves aggressiveness, stamina, and
courageous action in the face of danger. Adolescent boys are
required to display their wand-nat by engaging in whipping
contests called *buhe* that can leave them with lacerations,
torn ears, and bleeding welts. Again, any sign of weakness is
greeted with taunts and mockery.

Similarly, in the New Guinea highlands, among the Sam-
bia, boys also endure bloody whippings, flailings, beatings,
and other forms of terror stoically and silently.

Among the San of Southwest Africa, a peaceful culture,
boys must prove their manhood by tracking and killing an
adult antelope. The Native American Fox of Iowa, another
nonviolent tribe, refer to real manhood as the "Big Impossible"; it is only achieved through attainment of economic
success and tribal leadership.

Among most peoples it appears that manhood must be proved, by relating successfully—without loss of composure or competence—to stress and agony. Noted exceptions include the Tahitians of the South Seas and the Senai of Malaysia, who appear to have little sense of gender differentiation and tend to be under little stress from the natural or human environment, or, as with the Senai, they, for reasons unclear, fastidiously choose to avoid conflict.

COMPULSIVE MASCULINITY AND SEXISM

Compulsive masculinity is inexorably tied to sexism—in proving manhood a man is proving his superiority to women by enduring distress that women supposedly cannot endure. The domination and degradation of women are a basic defense used to bolster men's vulnerable masculinity. Where men are compulsively masculine, they are also sexist. What follows are some assumptions of sexist men, stated at their most extreme and stereotypical:[16]

Men and women are inherently different.

Real men are superior to women and superior to men who do not live up to models of masculinity.

Activities normally associated with women are demeaning for men to engage in.

Men should not feel or express vulnerable or sensitive emotions; the manly emotions are lust and anger.

Toughness and the domination of others are central to men's identity.

Sex is less about pleasure or relating and more about proving manhood and asserting power.

Gay men are failed men.

Relatively few men may actively express such beliefs; far more men feel them than express them. But it is safe to say that all men in American society must—to some degree—negotiate their identities by way of such ideas. I am struck by the powerful psychic resonance such ideas have for me, even though I do not intellectually subscribe to them. They are far more alive in my emotions than I would like them to be. For instance, I react with anxiety to the thought of engaging in certain "women's activities" like sewing; I still have trouble acknowledging, much less expressing, vulnerable emotions; the element of performance as an end in itself is still more alive in my sex life than I want it to be. And it has been a struggle to acknowledge the liberatory potential that gay men offer straight men.

I find it impossible to imagine compulsive masculinity without sexism. The inability to empathize with women, to experience "vulnerable" emotions, to engage in egalitarian sex, or to empathize with gays is tied to the need to prove manhood by never regressing under stress.

CHODOROW

Compulsive masculinity is a multidetermined phenomenon. Such things as the material conditions that stress a culture; the prevalence of war; the historical evolution of women in certain societies; the degree of industrialization; and, arguably, the way genetic predisposition combines with material stresses[17] all can contribute heavily to compulsive masculinity. If, for reasons of material survival, the men in a culture must perform difficult and dangerous acts, there will be a strong need for men to learn to endure danger stoically and for masculinity to be so defined. Or, if there is a significant chance a boy will eventually have to kill or risk being killed in war, compulsive masculinity will be strongly motivated.

What interests me is how psychological forces interact with such objective stresses and with stresses that may result from the advance of technology or changes in economic systems. (I am aware that causality moves in a circle in these matters.) I will initially offer a psychoanalytic feminist model that can be applied broadly and loosely to compulsive masculinity, but which, more specifically, addresses its psychological sources in American culture.

Psychoanalytic sociologist Nancy Chodorow offers a useful model for understanding personality differences in men and women. Her analysis revolves around certain psychic patterns that appear to result from being parented predominantly by a woman during early childhood—still the most common form of parenting. In early infancy, mother-raised boys and girls experience a certain psychological oneness, or "primary identification," with the mother in which the baby's identity is fused with the mother's. For my purposes, it doesn't matter whether such a pure identification exists; a strong feeling of identification and safety will serve my argument. In early life, in response to stress and distress, boys and girls seek safety through identification with mother; through repeating this identification thousands of times they come to internalize the feeling of safety. It is through burrowing in mother's arms and feeling a kind of tactile oneness that this is done. In identifying with mother, one sees the world through her eyes, and therefore one identifies with her attraction to father, while at the same time seeing her as a love object. (This has important implications for homophobia that I will explore in chapter 6.) Identification and attraction are key concepts: in identification one seeks to become the other; in attraction one seeks to possess the other.

As boys and girls separate from the mother, they have radically different developmental tasks. The little boy realizes that he will grow up to be a man and so must shift his identification to his father—a difficult, wrenching trial. His mother pushes him to identify with his father. In shifting identification, he will also shift some erotic attachment to his father; this he will learn is unacceptable and must be defended against. (Again see chapter 6.) The girl must shift her erotic attachment to her father while retaining her maternal identification. This shift is made easier because her identification with her mother is also an identification with her mother's attraction to father.

Because the father is typically absent or remote, the boy is said to identify *positionally* with a masculine position or role, or with grandiose stereotypes of masculinity offered by the culture. One can add that fathers are more likely to relate to the boy positionally, that is, through mediated identification with the masculine role, through engaging in "masculine" activities together. In contrast, the girl identifies *personally* with her largely present mother. (Again, I am describing the stereotypical nuclear family in which the mother does most of the childrearing.)

The father, in this model, is distant, physically remote, off at work, and often absent. The boy is likely to distort and glorify his father and identify with his distorted perception of his father's role, and with grandiose cultural stereotypes of masculinity. The boy's understanding of his father—and masculinity—is insufficiently constrained by his father's presence. The boy comes to define his masculinity negatively—as that which is not feminine; he attempts to repress his internalized primary identification and dependence on his mother. He both represses what he regards as feminine within himself and devalues what he perceives as feminine in the external world.

As a result, masculinity becomes a lifelong problem that is never completely resolved. The boy becomes accomplished

at separation and the denial of relationship; his ego boundaries are more rigid and less essentially relational than those
of a girl. The young girl, by contrast, identifies with a mother
who is present; her sense of herself as feminine is less likely
to be problematic.

The all-too-familiar man who is (1) deeply insecure about
his manhood and possesses an insatiable, compulsive need
to prove it, (2) homophobic and defends himself against homosexual desire, and (3) relates to women in a sexist fashion,
can be better understood in terms of Chodorow's model.

I want to add to this analysis by distinguishing five stages related to young boys' processes of gender awareness and
changing identifications with the mother. (My conception of
these stages is influenced by, though not explicitly derived
from, the extraordinary work of Elizabeth Young-Bruehl.[18])
In stage one, a state of primary identification, the boy experiences no awareness of separation from the mother. This
stage, if it truly exists at all, begins in the womb and carries
over into the first two months of life. In stage two, a state
of separation begins in which the boy is aware of sepa-
rateness but not of gender, either his own or that of others.
In stage three, the boy begins to be aware of gender but
is unaware that his mother's gender is different. In stage
four, the boy becomes aware of gender difference between
himself and his mother, but does not yet find this psychically
dangerous. In stage five, the mother's gender difference becomes a source of psychic danger as he still longs for iden-

tification with her—or the "pregendered" version of her—and engages in the process of shifting identification to the father. These stages, completed by the age of three, occur serially in time, but also overlay and interpenetrate each other psychically, evoking each other and continuing to live in the boy's psyche. As these stages progress, the degree of identification the boy experiences slowly diminishes. Notice that in stages one through three the boy is not aware he is identified with a woman when he seeks his mother's safety, and even in stage four the mother is a relatively safe object of identification.

I will return to these stages shortly.

FREUD

Freud's later model of neurotic anxiety offers a conceptually elegant way to clarify the psychic conflict at the heart of compulsive masculinity. In *Inhibitions, Symptoms and Anxiety,* Freud distinguished healthy anxiety from neurotic anxiety.[19] Healthy anxiety is a response to an external danger situation that may be physical or psychological. Soldiers going off to war, men thrown out of work, and children witnessing parental violence, all face objective situations where anxiety is appropriate and functional.

Neurotic anxiety, in contrast, is a response to an internal danger. The internal danger consists of the consequences of feeling (or acting upon) an "instinctual demand," which, for

Freud, merely means a strong desire. (Nothing inherently biological attaches to the notion of an instinctual demand.) To feel the strong desire would result in a threat to the integrity of the ego, the organized sense of "me-ness" or "I-ness" that everyone in varying degrees possesses. The threat of feeling the strong desire and the danger it represents signals anxiety to the ego.

To remove the ego from danger, people develop symptoms and inhibitions that substitute for, and satisfy, the strong desire, keeping it out of awareness. As Freud put it in *Inhibitions, Symptoms and Anxiety:* "It might be said that symptoms are created so as to avoid the generation of anxiety. But this does not go deep enough. It would be truer to say that symptoms are created to avoid a *danger situation* whose presence has been signaled by the generation of anxiety" (55).

Without the symptoms that satisfy and keep at a safe distance the strong desire, the dangerous internal situation will emerge.

Freud goes on to say: "We have also come to the conclusion that an instinctual demand often only becomes an (internal) danger because its satisfaction would bring on an external danger—that is because the *internal danger represents an external one*" (emphasis added) (94).

Neurotic anxiety is then, not always merely intrapsychic; it often has roots in wishes that, if expressed, would be psychologically or even physically dangerous because of the potential reaction of others. The ego is itself profoundly social in origin and derives from experiences of mutual recognition, so what it finds dangerous at any given time in history will be profoundly affected by culture. The shifting tensions of history will, in ways not yet well articulated, make strong desires more or less dangerous or acceptable; thus internal danger situations, and the symptoms and inhibitions that attempt to substitute for the unacceptable strong desire, will often shift historically and will need to be understood sociologically.

And at a certain age the ego (and superego) becomes gendered—as Chodorow and others have argued—quite tenuously so for boys in the process of shifting identification to the father. Now, putting Freud and Chodorow together, for compulsively masculine boys and men, the strong desire, which represents a danger situation against which they must defend themselves, is the desire to regress and seek safety and identification with their mothers—something they did thousands of times in the first two years of life when hungry, frightened, or in physical or psychic pain.

Giving in to the desire for maternal identification threatens boys' tenuous sense of self as masculine and threatens them with homoerotic desires—or at least eroticized perceptions of other males. If boys are identified with mother they see father through mother's eroticized eyes. And, past a certain age, if they act out their regression around others, they will be punished or ostracized. It is important to notice that the young child's identification with mother is itself a defense, filled with aggression, and that there is an inevitable feeling of rage against one experienced as so powerful and awesome.[20] This rage receives some of its outlet later on as sexism directed at women; it is also directed against the self in the masochistic suffering that proving manhood engenders. The latter is a secondary gratification of compulsive masculinity.

The symptoms, which are meant to satisfy the desire to regress, consist of what I have called compulsive masculinity, taking that which once caused them to regress and identify with mother—stress and distress—and conquering it, and thereby feeling more like men and more separate from their mothers. By taking precisely that which calls up in them the desire to regress—distress—and "taking it like a man" (that is, without regressing), they prove their manhood and their superiority to women, with whom they secretly long to identify. Compulsive masculinity in part attempts to disempower the mother by proving that one can handle distress without her—and that one can handle distress that she and women generally cannot handle.

I will suggest in the next chapter that sexual intercourse, perhaps more than anything else, constitutes a stress that contains echoes of infantile identification with mother, and thus evokes the desire to identify with women. For this reason it is experienced as psychologically dangerous for men.

Inhibitions are more pervasive and characterological than symptoms, and consist of an incapacity to experience certain emotions. The inhibitions men tend to form consist of a generalized toughness, an incapacity to experience, acknowledge, or identify with emotions that might encourage regression: particularly sadness, grief, and hurt. Men's reluctance to identify with "cuteness" or weakness is fueled by the fear of being nurtured, which is one manifestation of the fear of maternal identification.

When boys repress their identification with mother, they are repressing a whole mode of relating that is empathic and weakly bounded. Crying, in particular, is regressive because it is an infant's primal expression of need for the mother. Boys often torment each other when they cry because they perceive the crying boy as regressing toward identification with mother. To identify with him threatens their own masculinity. Boys in a group are often assessing each other for signs of maternal dependency. When it manifests, one beats it down, in others and one's self. Consider this passage from Henry Roth's *Call It Sleep*, where David, an eight-year-old, has just been beaten by other boys:

> Tears sprang to his eyes. He cowered.
> "He's cryin'!" they jeered.
> "Look ad im cryin'."
> "Waaa!"
> "Cry baby, cry baby suck yer mudder's tiddy!" one of them began.
> "Cry baby, cry baby, suck yer mudder's tiddy." The rest took up the burden.
> The tears streaming down his face, David groped his way blindly through them. They opened a gap to let him pass and then followed him still chanting.
> "Cry baby, cry baby, suck yer mudder's tiddy!" [21]

Male glory can be usefully seen as a kind of substitute for infantile safety. One "basks" in it as one did in mother's arms. It is the opposite of "sucking your mother's tiddy." One achieves it by behaving heroically, by conquering that which once most caused one to seek out mother's arms. And when one achieves male glory, one has successfully satisfied one's desire to regress and feels united with one's gender ideal of masculinity—an ideal that was born at that moment when mother's safety began to be called into question and one began to shift identification to father.

At the developmental moment when mother becomes an ambiguous source of psychic safety, a split develops in the ego as a gender ideal of masculinity is slowly born. Male glory briefly heals that split and makes the boy at one with himself and other men, insofar as other men are identified with the gender ideal. Male glory, because it unifies the psyche, echoes the infantile unity that existed before the shift in identification began.

Predictably, male glory lowers some of the inhibitions men develop to protect themselves against the need to regress. At the moment of greatest male glory—winning the Super Bowl, hitting a home run, scoring a touchdown— men are able to be openly affectionate with each other, to hug and pat each other more freely. Generally, when men are openly striving toward a masculine ideal, they feel safer to lower such inhibitions.

Any male activity that seeks to prove masculinity through

the enduring of stress, constitutes a kind of training in the art of resisting regression. A man reading the sports page and glorying in a player's performance is regressing in the form of a wish-fulfilling daydream; but his regression strengthens his capacity, when faced with distress, to resist the impulse to regress further. (See chapter 5.)

I want to return to the five stages of identification with the mother. I claimed earlier that boys react against a dangerous strong desire for maternal identification by becoming compulsively masculine. I want to offer a subtle distinction: what they long for is not so much identification with the mother, understood as a gendered being, but an earlier stage of fusion with the mother found at its strongest in the womb in stage one. Boys want the safety of fusing with their mothers, but this safety preexisted their awareness of, or identification with, gender. So, strictly speaking, it is a little misleading to say that boys possess a residual longing for, and fear of maternal identification, because they long for a being that preexisted gender distinctions. The mother they melded with before they became aware of gender is a radically different mother than the gendered mother they confront when they realize they are boys and need to disidentify.

Elizabeth Young-Bruehl believes that sexism, in its core motivation, draws upon a nostalgic longing for what she calls the "phallic mother"—the young boy's belief that his mother is of the same gender. This is equivalent to stage three, in which the boy is aware of gender but believes he shares the same gender with his mother. As Young-Bruehl puts it: "Sexism is propelled not by a desire for Difference but by nostalgic desire for Before Difference or denial of Difference . . . Sexism is also propelled by defeat—the inevitable defeat—of that nostalgia."[22]

On some level, sexist boys and men try to deny that women are different from men, according to Young-Bruehl; when this fails another kind of sexism emerges. It is not clear to me to what extent boys in stage three believe in the existence of a phallic mother, or how important this may be. But it seems to me that it is not a nostalgic longing for the phallic mother that drives sexism, so much as the longing for the pregendered safety of stages one and two. This is a safety grounded less in some belief in a mother with a phallus and more in a state where there is no awareness of gender at all. But, after the boy reaches stage five, and realizes his mother is a woman and he is a boy, that safety can only be found by way of what the boy now knows is maternal identification— with all its threats to masculine identity. This is felt as a kind of betrayal—one is cast out of a paradise with the recognition of gender difference, but what is longed for is not a phallic mother but a non-gendered fusion with what is *now* known to be the mother. The mother, now known to be a woman, is in the way of what the boy wants because she is of a different gender. And boys and men possess intense longings for the womb, but to get back to the womb they must go by way of identification with women. The conflict this creates is one force driving sexism.

It is worth recognizing that in talking about these early childhood psychic states we are reaching into the ineffable. Wittgenstein famously said that if a lion could talk we would not understand him. I take this to mean that a lion's intelligibility is so radically discontinuous from ours, so beyond the range of our access or contemplation, with its world grounded so strongly in smell and four legged walking and God knows what, that we would lack any shared frame of reference to communicate. Something like this holds for our contemplation of early childhood experience and the five stages I suggest. We can catch glimmers of memory, brief evocations, but it is, finally, from the inside at least, irretrievable. It is thus important to underscore the extraordinary intensity of distress (and pleasure) we all feel in the first two years of life—and the inaccessibility of such states to adults. As psychoanalyst Ernest Schachtel has suggested, infantile experience is at once too painful and too pleasurable—too intense—for adult humans to place in the cultural forms that memory requires.[23] So language breaks down. One can use words like "ecstasy," "infantile rage," and "maternal omnipotence" to evoke resonances of certain infantile psychic states, but we cannot finally represent such states to ourselves—although some are better than others at this. As Schachtel puts it:

The categories (or schemata) of adult memory are not
suitable receptacles for early childhood experiences and
therefore not fit to preserve these experiences and enable
their recall. The functional capacity of the conscious,
adult memory is usually limited to those experiences the
adult consciously is aware of and is capable of having (284).

MANHOOD RITUALS
AND TRAUMATIC IDENTIFICATION

I want to turn now to the painful manhood rituals I described earlier. It would be foolish to authoritatively claim
that some psychological essence inheres in the manhood rituals that appear to unite hundreds of diverse cultures—but
that caution ought not to prevent creative speculation.

The manhood rituals I have mentioned for the most part
have in common older men inflicting severe physical pain or
distress on young men and forcing them to remain stoic to
prove manhood.[24] (I acknowledge that, from the point of
view of the older men, a difficult gift and responsibility is
being given.) The psychoanalytic feminist model I've put
forth adequately explains this phenomenon. But to gain a
deeper understanding of the relation between the experience
of pain and the identification with masculinity, I will draw
upon some ideas from existentialist thought.

Intense anxiety, as various existentialist thinkers have argued, is not just a feeling among other feelings, but rather
the threat of dissolution of the sense of self. The opposite of

anxiety is identity, as Herbert Fingarette has argued.[25] Anxiety is the threat of meaninglessness, nonbeing, chaos, disorganization; the threat of the loss of psychological and cultural intelligibility. Too much anxiety, and one goes crazy and enters a realm of chaos. And, arguably, the ultimate dissolution is dissolution back to identification with mother in the womb. It seems to me an open question whether, since severe distress and anxiety generally throw men's masculinity into question but not women's femininity, anxiety itself is experienced differently by men and women. If anxiety, whatever its trigger or object, threatens regressive dissolution back to mother for both men and women, then it will threaten identity in different ways, since such regression for men includes loss of gender. This is not to say that all anxiety for men is thematically *about* gender, but that gender may be implicated in anxiety for men in a way it is not for women.

Grueling manhood rituals simultaneously threaten identity in two ways that are only conceptually distinct: they force boys to remain competent while enduring severe physical pain, and they create a situation that evokes severe anxiety for psychological reasons. They can be seen as attempts to *traumatize* boys into identification with masculinity.

Severe physical distress, coupled with the injunction to act competently, brings one into an "existential" situation, a situation where one's guides, identities, essences, and tacitly held background definitions of self and world, begin to recede; the armature of the ego, which brought one into the situation, begins to weaken and one is left struggling for identity. Who one is and what one is doing are thrown into question by the need to continue on in the face of severe physical distress.

The pain generates an intense desire to cry out for mother's comfort, to identify with mother's safety, which one has internalized; but the consequences of such an act would be devastating. The boy knows that to do this would mark him for life as less than a man. This creates enormous anxiety and a traumatic identity crisis. It is a testing ground: one's strong desire to identify with mother is deliberately evoked and arduous suffering must be properly endured so that other men will perceive one as—and allow one to perceive one's self as—a man.

The rituals appear to attempt to obliterate any vestiges of one's identification with mother and then force one to identify with manhood. They look like one enormous counter-phobic reaction formation.

It is not surprising that, often, only after undergoing these rituals that men are considered ready to marry or have sex with women. It is as if having sex with women threatens men with regression; they must, through drastic measures, be assured of their manhood first.

Brutal manhood rituals set in relief what is too common for men in many western cultures: boys are brutalized into their identities as men. The process of "toughening" may be gradual or more sudden; it may serve objective ends that benefit a culture; but it is always motivated in part by flight from mother.

COMPULSIVE MASCULINITY AS EMOTION WORK—
FEELING RULES AND MANHOOD

In our private lives we frequently work hard to make our-selves feel what we want to feel, or believe we are supposed to feel: we give ourselves pep talks when we are depressed; we talk ourselves out of falling in love; we decide to let go and grieve over a loss; we work at liking our in-laws; we choose to have fun at a party. And at ceremonial occasions like funerals and weddings we adjust our moods as necessary. Function-ing tolerably in the world requires an array of interior ma-neuvers that Arlie Hochschild calls *emotion work*.[26] Hoch-schild argues that, in the twentieth century as automation has taken over the task of producing goods, more and more people work at jobs in which a service is provided to a pub-lic. Workers in such jobs are often required to induce or sup-press feeling in order to create a desired emotional state in those being serviced: a waitress affects charm and pleasant-ness around harassing customers; a therapist projects com-passion toward an irritating client; a nurse contrives sympa-thy for an obnoxious patient; a salesman expresses the same "heartfelt" enthusiasm for a product many times a day. Hochschild calls such paid emotion work emotional labor.

Compulsive masculinity can be understood as a form of structured, developmental, emotion work in the service of gender. To move from being a young baby who cries freely over distress and easily expresses need of mother, to a strong, silent man prepared for any emergency requires

an immense amount of emotion work repeated throughout childhood. Hochschild distinguishes surface acting, in
which one puts on a display of emotion, from deep acting, in
which one brings one's self to feel—or not feel—an emotion. The emotion work required to "become a man" consists of deep acting, and it follows what Hochschild calls *feeling rules:* don't feel fear, don't feel grief, don't feel sad, remain
cool under stress. And cultural forms of masculinity require
following these rules. Learning to walk, talk, sit, stand, and
act like a man means learning to work on your emotions
until you have achieved a degree of inhibition so that such
emotion work is no longer consciously necessary. Masculinity, a cultural construct, becomes internalized in one's body,
brain, and nervous system. If certain emotions threaten self-
esteem, then one works not to feel them—at great injury to
the self.

SOCIAL PSYCHOLOGY: MALE GLORY AND THREATS TO MEN'S SELF-ESTEEM

Social psychology, which contains a wealth of challenging
insight, has been insufficiently acknowledged in feminist
writings; I want to bring to bear some of its useful findings.

It is a mistake to view sexism (or racism, nationalism, or
any ingroup/outgroup prejudice) as a variation from some
true, underlying human nature. The need to identify with an
ingroup and see an outgroup as inferior, and to act accord-

ingly, appears deeply rooted in human beings and manifests itself even when group links are tenuous.

Social psychologist Henri Tajfel, in some remarkable much replicated experiments, has tried to establish what he calls *minimal groups*—groups formed on the basis of the most arbitrary, minimally significant similarities.[27] Such groups are created experimentally and share the following features:

> The members are all strangers to each other.
>
> The members are not in economic competition.
>
> It is clear to the members that they have been placed together randomly; for instance, through the flip of a coin.
>
> The members have no history of ill will among them.
>
> The members have no expectation of future interaction or competition—no stake in a common future.

Tajfel expected that minimal groups would not form stereotypes of each other or establish ingroup/outgroup contexts—he expected no prejudice or "group-ism." What he found was the opposite. People in minimal group situations formed positive images of their own groups and negative images of other groups. This extended to their "institutional" behavior. When they were asked to grade people for performing small tasks, subjects showed significant prejudice and favoritism toward members of their own groups. In addition, they were more likely to engage in group-serving attributions. When someone in their own group made a mistake, they were more likely to attribute it to external, noncharacterological causes ("He did not get enough sleep last night; anyone would have made that mistake.") When someone in the outgroup made a mistake, they were more likely to attribute it to internal, characterological causes ("He is lazy. He is not as bright.")

Even in the most arbitrarily based groups, prejudice and even institutional ingroup favoritism, akin to institutional racism or sexism, formed and distorted the capacity of people to fairly evaluate the competence of others.

Tajfel's much replicated findings, along with the fact that all known cultures engage in forms of ingroup/outgroup prejudice, suggest how deeply rooted in our natures outgroup prejudice is. In most cultures of the world, it is a part of every male's conditioning to view females as the Other and to glory in manhood. Sexism differs from most outgroup prejudice in that the outgroup consists of people one is raised by, loves, and regularly is close to. (Thus, psychodynamic analyses are relevant to sexism in a way they may not be for other outgroup prejudices.)

In other words, the starting point for self-reflection about any prejudice is to notice how deeply rooted ingroup/outgroup prejudice is in humans—how readily we identify with a group and see another group as "them."

If prejudice is a natural human tendency, then receiving hits to our self-esteem can intensify the effect, causing us to glorify our ingroup and denigrate outgroups. Robert Cialdini gave undergraduates at Arizona State University a bogus creativity test. He told half the students that they had failed

the test; he told the others nothing about their performance.[28] Then he asked all of them to compare Arizona
State with their rival school, the University of Arizona, on a
number of characteristics. Students who had taken a hit to
their self-esteem—being told they had failed a creativity
test—praised Arizona State and were far more critical of the
University of Arizona than students told nothing about their
test results.

No logical connection exists between loss of self-esteem
and one's evaluation of the two universities; but the psychological link is strong. The pain of losing self-esteem can be
coped with by fleeing into psychic acts of identification that
artificially raise self-esteem. Fantasy serves to replace the
self-esteem that has been lost in reality. So the "injured" students gloried in Arizona State and felt superior to the University of Arizona, which they belittled. Cialdini's findings
are much replicated ones. The students engaged in what is
known as BIRGing—basking in reflected glory, feeling that
"we" are better than "they" by our association with an insti-
tution. (Any man who reads the sports page—a form of institutionalized BIRGing—will understand. See chapter 5.)

Compulsive masculinity is about the pursuit of self-
esteem; the desire to regress, to experience "feminine" emotions, constitutes a built-in internal threat to boys' and men's
self-esteem. Certain basic human emotions—especially grief
and fear—are experienced as internal threats to self-esteem
by boys seeking separation from their mothers. Other boys
displaying such emotions, like crying or cowering in fear,

awaken such psychically intolerable threats, and so are thus targets of attack.

When self-esteem is internally threatened, boys flee into BIRGing and grandiosity—witness the attraction to grandiose masculinity found in most boys and its lingering effects in men. BIRGing is usually thought of as gaining esteem through showing off connections with successful others. Learning to be a man is learning to gain esteem through a form of self-presentation that associates one with ideals of manhood. Masculinity is pervaded with BIRGing. Freud argued that groups are held together through shared identification with ego ideals.[29] When everyone in a group identifies with the same ego ideal, they identify with each other. I think he was mostly talking about men. Fathers tend to bond with sons, and men and boys with each other through mediated, positional identification—shared activity by which they implicitly identify with ideals of masculinity. It is an identification not through explicit fantasy but through activity framed ("cathected") by fantasy. The much remarked fragility and absurdity of the male ego, which so readily make men figures of fun, is rooted in men's tenuous self-esteem, which results in BIRGing and glory seeking.

EMPIRICAL CONFIRMATION

My analysis of compulsive masculinity is structural in nature; it says nothing about the genetic endowment of a particular man or genetics' role in personality; it says nothing about who the parents are, their class, racial or ethnic identity, what "values they transmit," or the presence of extended family, active in childrearing and able to provide greater psychic fluidity to children, all of which is of great importance. My model is in no way comprehensive; I present it as one take on men. My argument—an old one in feminist circles—is that who does the parenting is important. Any rigorous attempt to confirm the foregoing ideas will have to consider the many potentially confounding variables that might encourage compulsive masculinity.

It is beyond the scope of this book to comprehensively examine the social science evidence and clinical observations that might tend to elucidate the sources of compulsive masculinity. Relatively little research has been done on this. But I want to briefly suggest what we might expect from such research. Empirical social science, anthropological data, and clinical and personal observation ought to roughly confirm the following:

> Those cultures with prolonged maternal dependence have more severe rites of passage to masculinity and more compulsive masculinity. Any such research must allow for the confounds of material stress.

> Within American culture, where fathers are absent and mothers do most of the child-rearing, one would expect to find more compulsive masculinity among individual boys and men.

> Compulsively masculine men have greater homophobia.

COMPULSIVE MASCULINITY
AND THE REPRESSION OF HUMAN VIRTUES

I said earlier that many forms of evil are implicated in the at-tempts of men to prove manhood. It ought to be clear that the formation of compulsively masculine, sexist men, injures their humanity, which in turn causes them to injure others. The repression of, and hostility toward, the pre-oedipal mother causes men, as Eli Sagan puts it, "to downgrade the moral virtues we all learn from that same pre-oedipal mother: nurturance, pity, compassion, love, conscience. No repression of women is possible without the repression of these great virtues as well." [30]

3

Pornography, Sexism, and Male Heterosexuality

One realm where manhood is threatened and proved is the realm of sexuality; this has become visible in recent years in discussions of pornography. In pornography debates, three views mingle and collide like bits of mercury forced together: feminist struggles against sexism and violence against women; liberal (and sometimes feminist) aspirations toward sexual openness, freedom, and tolerance; and reactionary fears of sex. We are asked to be (1) outraged at the sexism in men's minds and its ubiquitous dissemination in pornography and its inexorable expression in violence toward women, (2) grateful that we can finally honestly acknowledge, and freely explore and express, our sexuality, and (3) appalled at the presence of "such filth" in our community. I take the first view very seriously, the second somewhat less so, and the third not at all, though I think the third nudges and constrains me in visceral, semiconscious ways.

Pornography (by which, for the purposes of this chapter, I denote the varieties of heterosexual visual pornography found in American pornography stores) offers some of the most vivid, sensational, and widely accessible manifestations of sexism and misogyny to be found in U.S. culture. This is not to say that all men who use, or could be excited by pornography, are necessarily sexist or misogynist in their actions; it would be comparably outrageous to argue that women who are excited by sadomasochistic pornography want to be treated in a sexist or misogynous fashion. I wonder whether in a culture with little or no sexist action or violence against women, pornography might exist without protest against its sexism. Given that men can be antisexist yet excited by sexist pornography, a world where men were antisexist yet enjoyed pornography seems psychologically conceivable.

In what follows I attempt to shed light on heterosexual men and their visual experience of women, their sexual distress, their difficulty identifying with women's experience, and their use of pornography. Since I seek to understand certain forms of male suffering, which I take to be real *and* which men use to justify sexism and rape, I want to be clear: to understand or even empathize with someone's distress is not to legitimate what it is used to justify, or what may appear to issue from it. Any attempt to understand male sexual distress must be undertaken with an eye to gaining insight as to how men might finally stop doing the horrible things they do—to women, to each other, and to themselves. The ultimate "solution" to the "problem" of pornography is to stop sexism and violence against women, and thereby render pornography irrelevant. Sex could then be a domain free to express itself without being perceived through the oppressions of gender.

It is worth repeating here that I am writing about heterosexual visual pornography—magazines mostly. I have seen few pornography films.

INTRUSIVE IMAGES

Pornography cannot be fully understood apart from men's daily social experience of looking at women. I want to distinguish four kinds of men's visual experience of women and women's bodies: authorized images, stolen images, intrusive images, and authorized stolen images.[1]

Authorized images are those one is socially authorized to look at. A man is socially authorized to look at a painting of a nude woman in a museum, a nude statue, or a woman's face in a personal interaction. Male judges judging bathing beauty contests, male gynecologists doing pelvic examinations, and male art students painting a nude female model, are all authorized to look at women's bodies in certain predefined, prescribed ways.

But if a man stares at the crotch of a nude statue or painting, or at the breasts of a woman during a social interaction—or if the gynecologist, judge, or art student look lustfully at what he is authorized to see—the image becomes *stolen.* Notice that stolen images come in two forms: looking at something one is not authorized to look at and looking lustfully at what one is authorized to look at. And there are images that men are authorized, indeed expected, to notice, but are not authorized to stare at: a woman's cleavage in a low-cut dress, the legs of a woman in a miniskirt. And, as I have suggested, there are images one is authorized neither to notice nor to look at: the faintly visible underwear of a woman sitting while wearing a short skirt. Stealing images of women's bodies is a troubled activity that pervades many heterosexual men's adolescent and postadolescent social experience. A fifteen-year-old boy sitting bored in a classroom notices the inner thigh of a girl sitting across the room; he is titillated and wants to look but feels socially prohibited from staring. So he may present what Erving Goffman calls a "body gloss." Through bodily signification, a body gloss helps free him from the undesirable, characterological implications of what he finds himself doing. Sample body glosses: a man standing on a suburban sidewalk late at night waiting for a ride casts exaggerated glances down the street to signify his reason for being there; a man lifting a heavy object around others exaggerates his grunts and groans to mask his actual difficulty and vulnerability in lifting the object. And our fifteen-year-old boy scans his eyes in the direction of the girl's thighs, avoiding staring, allowing himself to catch only an occasional glimpse, or he solemnly stares in her vicinity as if lost in thought while keeping her thighs in the barely accessible periphery of his visual field. It's a skill many boys learn. (Nude beaches and restaurants with topless waitresses are places where people, authorized to notice but not to stare, selectively disattend erotic images and use glosses to mask staring. As Goffman puts it, "When bodies are naked, glances are clothed."[2]) Stealing images and glossing the activity are deeply humiliating and isolating for men, not in the ways that striking out with the bases loaded or dropping a pass in the end zone are consciously, acutely humiliating, but rather as a chronic, fearful, humiliated stance toward women that often pervades men's daily social experience of sexual longing. This activity is humiliating because it is desperate and outcast, because one works so hard for so little, and, perhaps above all, because it shuts one out from social mutuality.

Part of the social prohibition on sexual looking is both reflected and perpetuated by a central metaphor for seeing in English: Seeing is touching. We say that a woman could "feel a man's eyes on her"; his eyes were "glued to her"; he "ran his eyes all over her body."[3] Marshall McLuhan is reported by Tom Wolfe to have cleverly invoked this metaphor of the gaze as physical contact while having dinner at a topless restaurant: "These women aren't nude," said McLuhan. "They're wearing *us*."

Intrusive images is a category more personal than social;

variations in personality will cause images to feel intrusive to some but not others. I distinguish three types of intrusive images then: ordinary intrusive images; arousing intrusive images that require a prior condition of need to arouse; and arousing intrusive erotic images.

Some ordinary intrusive images: an alarm going off, the bright lights of a passing car hurting one's eyes; a twenty dollar bill seen on the sidewalk; flashing neon signs; tiny hairs scratching and stinging one's skin after a haircut; sudden physical pain.

Arousing intrusive images: The smell of pizza wafting from a restaurant is smelled by a hungry person passing by on the sidewalk; a person trying to quit caffeine smells coffee; an eighteen-year-old eager to buy his or her first car is distracted by a TV commercial for cars.

I will only discuss arousing intrusive erotic images that are felt by heterosexual men: a woman's nipples seen through her blouse, the thighs of a woman wearing a miniskirt, or the smell of perfume worn by an ex-lover. Advertising is full of images of women that are likely to catch men unaware, either by providing a sexy image of a woman to favorably associate a product with sex or by showing how a woman might seek to use it. I counted nine potentially intrusive erotic images in this morning's paper, most of them associated with advertising. Sexually attractive women in and of themselves can clearly be felt by men as intrusive; what begins as an intrusive image may then become a stolen one. Images can be simultaneously stolen and intrusive; one feels an image intruding into one's field of vision and is authorized to notice but not to stare at, so one steals. Talking to a woman wearing a sexy low-cut dress, a man may experience her breasts as intrusive and cast stolen glimpses at them. A kind of power struggle may ensue in the man as he attempts to dominate and "defuse" the intrusive image. It is extraordinary the degree to which whole industries exist to make women's presence feel potentially intrusive and arousing to men; women's makeup, perfume, jewelry, and clothes are all in varying degrees attempts at this.

In the last fifty years we have seen a massive dissemination of erotic images in advertising, contrived with increasing skill to distract, arouse, and awaken male sexual feeling. While psychoanalysis has sought to integrate and demystify disowned fragments of the self through making explicit the meaning of sexual (and other) dreams, images, and fantasies, consumer culture generally, and advertising in particular, has done the reverse.[4] Erotic images in advertising exploit half-conscious, unintegrated feelings and needs through subliminal or semiconscious arousal. In television advertising, this is sometimes done with extraordinary rapidity and subtlety. The result is a vague, amorphously directed sexual resentment of women and resentment of sexual desire itself. Men feel stimulated against their will, hence powerless, distracted, and resentful.

In interviewing men on the subject of rape, in one form or another I often heard men (not rapists) say: "I have been injured by women. By the way they look, move, smell, and behave they have forced me to have sexual sensation I didn't want to have. If a man rapes a sexy woman, he is forcing her to have sexual sensation she doesn't want. It is just revenge." The view of a woman's appearance as a weapon, or at least as a powerful physical force, is metaphorically structured in English. A sexy woman is a *bombshell,* a *knockout, dressed to kill,* a *femme fatale, devastating, ravishing, striking,* or *stunning.* (While in "seeing is touching," seeing is understood as an active intervention, seeing is understood here as being passively acted upon.) Consider the overwhelming intrusiveness implicit in those words, and the disruptiveness suggested by three men's comments:

> Growing up, I definitely felt teased by women. I think for the most part women knew I was attracted to them so women would sit a certain way or give a three-quarter beaver shot or give you a little bit of tit and maybe not give much more, or lift their skirts a certain way. I definitely felt played with, used, manipulated, like women were testing their power over me. I hated it with a passion! With a *fucking* passion! Stan, 34, construction worker.[5]

> When you see a girl walking around wearing real skimpy clothes, she's offending you . . . .

> When you have a steady girlfriend or if you're married, girls will flirt with you to give you that enraged temptation. They know you're not going to do anything to them, so they're going to push real hard to make you real mad. Joe, 19, college student (54–55).

Where I work it's probably no different from any other major city in the U.S. The women dress up in high heels and they wear a lot of makeup, and they just look really hot and really sexy and how can somebody who has a healthy sex drive not feel lust for them?

I feel they have power over me just by their presence. Just the fact that they can come up to me and just melt me and make me feel like a dummy makes me want revenge. Jay, 23, file clerk (42–44).

I want to underscore two points that I will return to later. These men experience intrusive images and the process of stealing images as both injurious to their self-esteem and sexually frustrating. Such feelings are not uncommon in men. The magazine *Men's Health* surveyed 444 readers, 97 percent of whom were men, on women's sexual harassment of men in the workplace.[6] Forty-nine percent said there were women in their offices whose dress was "pointedly provocative"; 33 percent of the respondents believed men should report such women for sexual harassment. Consider: a third of these men believe a man is being seriously, legally sexually harassed by a woman on the job if she simply looks sexy and dresses sexily!

Such feelings are by no means confined to the uneducated. William Muehl, a retired professor at the Yale Divinity School, wrote in a June 12, 1992, letter to the *New York Times:* "The way young women dress in the spring constitutes a sexual assault upon every male within eyesight of them."

A deep feeling of injustice can be found in some men about the relation between stolen and intrusive images, one that I have never heard explicitly expressed. It goes roughly like this:

> Women not only have the right to, but often work hard to make themselves look sexy and to distract, disrupt, and intrude upon me just by their presence; yet if I notice something sexy about a woman, I have to mask my need to look and furtively steal glimpses. Either way I'm humiliated. If they have the right to intrude, I should have the right to look. But I don't.

When men as a group harass a passing woman they are, among other things, seeking revenge against women for the humiliation they feel they have suffered yet have difficulty acknowledging; they are unconsciously attempting to remedy a perceived injustice about their right to look. They are also bonding around some superior shared ideal of masculinity that enables them to view women as objects to be degraded.

Intrusive images help create unwanted (or ambivalently wanted) erections in adolescents and other men; the experience of having, hiding, and getting rid of such erections is humiliating and sometimes shaming. One may attempt to hide one's arousal physically or mask it through appearing solemn or overly vigilant in doing what one is supposed to be doing. (High school classrooms are a common domain where this occurs.) But when a male adolescent attempts to think and feel his way out of an erection, he engages in a process much deeper than body glossing, a process I described in chapter 2 as emotion work.[7] Emotion work is the work of making oneself feel (or not feel) particular emotional states to satisfy the demands of a social or personal circumstance. It is deeper, more basic work than the work of simply signifying or presenting an outward appearance of emotion.

The emotion work of getting rid of an erection is difficult to describe. The simplest description: one relaxes, disattends sexual stimulation, goes about one's business, and lets the erection go away by itself. Actively positive, or autosuggestive, thinking may or may not help. The emotion work of getting rid of erections is something most boys learn or try to learn. Consider this progression: A boy is "struck" by an intrusive erotic image, say, the sight of a girl's thighs and underwear across a classroom; he casts masked, stolen glances at the image; he finds himself becoming erect and enjoys the erection until he starts to feel self-conscious; he engages in the emotion work of getting rid of the erection; that night he calls upon the image in fantasy while masturbating; and the image becomes part of his "image repertoire," visual property to be called upon for arousal and gratification at another time. He has suffered humiliation by the image and, in a sense, conquered it by gaining control over it and perhaps in the process gained control over the relation between images, erections, and orgasms. One of the functions of masturbation is to get training in the emotion work of controlling erections, and controlling the relation between image and arousal. This relation is intensified by the disruptive experience of wet dreams, in which one controls neither the image nor the orgasm.

Intrusive images can be more or less simply pleasurable and incur no resentment in men. But their effect on many male psyches is to create stress, distress, and a longing for relief and control—a longing that pornography ministers to. Pornographic images in varying degrees are both authorized and stolen but generally not intrusive; one is authorized to pull out a centerfold in one's bedroom, but not, at least not quite yet, in a restaurant or on a bus. "Society at large" defines pornographic images as stolen, but the framing of pornographic images and the content of the images themselves attempt to authorize men to look, fantasize, and masturbate. Consider *Playboy:* Hugh Hefner produced a whole industry replete with a "philosophy," special clubs, emblems, books, a magazine, a grant-giving organization, a palace, and a TV show, all more or less to authorize men to look at nude women.

By being really three magazines—one for intellectuals, one for consumers, and one for masturbation—*Playboy* sought to cushion men's distress over looking at women's bodies. And the facial expressions and body postures of the women posed were meant to make men feel proud in looking. The essence of pornography is to offer men arousal and gratification without vulnerability, without risk to the self. For male adolescents, looking at women is full of risk in the form of humiliation, desperation, and sexual distress. Since masturbation itself is often experienced as risky, ambiguously approved of by the world, and a sign of failure, pornography must cushion its implicit risk.

I suspect that the more men feel victimized by intrusive images, the more they will need pornographic images; and that intrusive images, because they are experienced as nonconsensual by so many men, are more likely to encourage men to justify violence against women than is pornography, which although often sexist, is at least felt as consensual.[8] Much pornography strikes me as a kind of revenge against women's putative capacity to arouse through appearing sexy, revenge against the pain caused by intrusive and stolen images, revenge against women's sexiness itself. (Male lust is often felt as vengeful.) Pornography is a kind of prop that attempts to offer training in the emotion work of attaining sexual arousal and gratification while feeling proud and feeling little identification with women.

Radical feminists have argued that pornography, more than being the mere depiction of the degradation or subordination of women, *actually* degrades and subordinates women. Many people find this formulation problematic. How can pictures do more than depict? How can they actually degrade or subordinate? The answer lies in seeing that in our social practices we have many symbolic methods of degrading or celebrating people and classes of people.[9] I think the formulation is correct for much (but not all) of pornography. I would amend it to say: Much pornography degrades and subordinates "sexy" women or sexiness in women. Some pornography seems ambiguous in this regard, complex and difficult to classify in terms of social celebration or degradation.

A brief comparison of pornography with the male sports media may be instructive. Within the context of our social practices, the male sports media—that is, the sports page, sports magazines, televised and radio broadcasts of male sports—serve not merely to report or make accessible sporting events. Rather, they also serve to celebrate, honor, and *super* ordinate the class of athletically skilled men. They help male consumers of sports feel more manly, proud, and in certain respects, superior to women through helping men to vicariously identify with men of extraordinary physical skill.

Much pornography attempts to help men feel manly and proud through feeling aroused by, and superior to, sexy women. Thus pornography subordinates and degrades sexy women, not, as I will argue, through treating women as bodies without consciousness, but through treating them as bodies given stereotyped subjectivities that encourage men to feel superior.

SUBJECTIFIED BODIES

"Objectification" may be the central concept in the feminist critique of pornography. Pornography is often decried for presenting women as mere objects or things, and for encouraging men to so regard them. As Susan Griffin puts it:

> At the very core of the pornographic mise-en-scène is the concept of woman as object. A woman's body forms the center of a magazine. She spreads apart her thighs and stares into the camera. Her tongue licks her lips. *Her eyes reflect back nothing;* she *is not human.* . . . She wears white sheer stockings . . . white pearls. . . . She is decorated in whiteness. In her image all the meanings of absence are realized. Her "whiteness" opens out to a *blank space in the mind.* . . . For the pornographic camera performs a miracle in reverse. Looking on a living being, a person with a soul, it produces an image of a *thing* (emphasis added).[10]

And Laura Lederer and Diana Russell attack nonviolent pornography on similar grounds:

> Not all pornography is violent but even the most banal pornography objectifies women's bodies. An essential ingredient of much rape and other forms of violence is the objectification of the woman. This is not just rhetoric. It means that women are not *seen* as human beings but as *things* (emphasis added).[11]

I have learned a great deal from Griffin, Lederer, and Russell—their work opened my eyes to the sexism in pornography. But it seems to me that their views, on one reading at least, miss something central about pornography—the crucial importance to men of the presented subjectivity of the women in pornographic images. The notion that pornography teaches men to view women as objects or things has, roughly speaking, at least two disparate, sometimes conflicting, meanings. An object or thing differs from a person in two relevant ways. First, an object lacks autonomy and is treated as such, that is, it is meant to be used for one's purposes. Second, an object lacks subjectivity or consciousness and is so experienced (and is thus to be "used" in the first sense). The "use" sense of objectifying differs significantly from the "lacks subjectivity" sense of objectifying. Griffin, Russell, and Lederer seem to believe that through denying women's subjectivity in the depiction of women, pornography encourages men to use women sexually without respecting their autonomy.

But notice some of the ways that men use women sexually and the wide range of acknowledgment of women's subjectivity that can accompany them:

1. A rapist projects false subjectivity onto a woman and scares her into "consent," rapes her, then asks for a date. A not uncommon phenomenon.
2. A rapist with exaggerated vigilance accurately attends a woman's subjectivity, perceptively identifying her moods and maneuvers as she seeks emotional and physical survival.
3. A rapist minimally notices a woman's subjectivity and physically overpowers her.
4. An intelligent, articulate, perceptive, sexist, "classically bastard" man scrupulously attends to a woman's subjec-

tive state—listening well, commenting perceptively, signifying a nonexistent concern, and making her feel "understood"—in order to gain consent. After the conquest, he evinces little interest in her.

Readers can make up their own examples. Using a woman sexually can and often does involve a wide range of acknowledgment of the woman's subjectivity. Treating people as if they lacked feelings ("using them like a Styrofoam cup and then discarding them") is not the same as *experiencing* them as if they had no feelings, or not perceiving their feelings. A man can objectify a woman while remaining attentive to her subjectivity. In using pornography, as in masturbating using one's own fantasies and images, men certainly *use* images of women, and the images of women themselves will "contain" varying degrees and kinds of subjectivity.

But what of the stronger claim that pornographers depict, and men view, women in pornography as things or objects lacking subjectivity or consciousness? This view strikes me as mistaken for two reasons. First, it is extremely difficult for a person in Western culture to look upon the human body—especially the face—without investing it with subjectivity. (Eye doctors work hard to cultivate a posture in which they can filter out the eye's signification as a subjective gaze and examine the eye clinically.) Just as it is difficult to experience the food we eat as possessing subjectivity (gingerbread men and animal crackers aside), it is a part of our preintentional acculturated stance toward live human bodies, or images of such, to experience them as subjects. Such a stance is "sedi-mented" in our nervous system; it is how bodies "show up" for us, temporally and phenomenologically prior to our particular thoughts and beliefs about women and their bodies.

My second objection to the view that pornography empties women of subjectivity is that a central ingredient in the sexual charge of most pornography, and in the work and motivation of the pornographer, is to present women's bodies that signify subjectivities that either are sexually exciting to men, or that make men comfortable looking at or masturbating to the image, or both. Pornography does not so much turn women into objects or things; rather it turns them into narrowly *subjectified bodies.* In a pornography store, one is inundated with images of women's bodies conveying stereotyped subjectivities: women as lusty, fearful, alluring, childlike, coy, trusting, hardy, compliant, mean, resistant, and so forth. But above all, *subjectivities:* unclad women unambiguously signifying certain psychic states to fit men's fantasies or cushion men's egos. And the subjectivity signified is inseparable from the body, its posture, and most of all, facial expression. Part of fantasizing (or actualizing) using a woman's body for pleasure involves using the body's subjectivity, that is, the woman's imagined experience of pleasure (or whatever). It is my impression that when focusing on a woman's body in masturbation, whether pornography-aided or not, the commonest subjectivity projected on the woman is strong sexual heat, and that men's own sexual excitement fuses with that imagined for the woman's body; indeed the particular image of the body is chosen because it can signify sexual heat.

It may be asked: What of men who have sex with inflatable dolls or mannequins? Do they project subjectivity onto their "partners" during sex? My hunch is that they seek the tactile and visual simulacra of sex with none of the hassle and anxiety of dealing with an actual person; they are free to project any subjectivity they wish, within the constraints of the inexorable preexistent significations of their "partners."

John Berger, writing about the history of painting, makes a useful distinction between the naked and the nude:

> To be naked is to be oneself.
> To be nude is to be seen naked by others and yet not recognized for oneself. . . . Nakedness reveals itself. Nudity is placed on display.
> To be naked is to be without disguise.
> To be on display is to have the surface of one's own skin, the hairs of one's own body, turned into a disguise. Nudity is a form of dress.[12]

And for Berger, the point of the nude "form of dress" is to project a certain subjectivity that flatters the painting's probable male viewers. In my terms, the "nude" is a form of sophisticated, stylized subjectification of women's bodies. The "naked," the woman painted or photographed as herself, also occurs in pornography; for example, in pornographic films in which a couple is enjoying each other sexually despite the presence of lights and camera, the woman and man may be honestly expressing their subjective states. (Although men viewing this may still project a distorted subjectivity onto the woman.)

In *Playboy's Women of the World*[13] I count 149 pictures of unclad women; 148 are subjectified bodies; one (mysteriously included) is a picture of a woman who happens to be without clothes, being herself. What distinguishes her from the other 148? In the 148 subjectified bodies, the two main signifiers of subjectivity, facial expression and body posture, both are composed to be viewed by men; their subjectivity is a complement to their viewability as bodies. It must be seen to be understood—compare a picture from a nudist magazine with a *Playboy* centerfold. It isn't that the Playboy body lacks subjectivity and the naked woman being herself possesses it; rather the fact of her nude body defines the subjectivity of the subjectified body; the felt mood of the naked woman being herself defines her subjectivity.

It is this overdefining of subjectivity that constitutes some of the most egregious sexism of pornography. Nothing sexist *inheres* in the visual presentation of unclad women. (Although some men can only relate to such an image in a sexist fashion.) It is pornography's encouraging of men to possess a distorted knowledge of women's subjectivity that is sexist. For most heterosexual men, being attracted to a woman means, in part, being excited by her body; what is sexist is the inability to simultaneously feel that while acknowledging and respecting her person.

Two motives for the particular subjectification of women's bodies are to excite and, in varying degrees, to flatter, comfort, and give pride to men. These two motives blend in pornography and may be only conceptually distinct. But, clearly, women's subjectivity is presented in an attempt to turn masturbation and looking at women's bodies into a *proud* experience. Male masturbation to pornography is fraught with shame for several reasons: It suggests one's failure as a man to get a real woman; it involves looking at an image of a sexy nude woman, an activity potentially fraught with humiliation in actual experience when stealing, or feeling intruded upon by sexy images; it involves an absence of mutuality; it evokes a lingering folk heritage of degradation—masturbation can give one warts, insanity, or blindness—connected to puritanical impulses; it has for over twenty years been decried as sexist by feminists. Given this context of shame, one task of the visual pornographer is to make the male viewer feel superior and to authorize men to look.

THE FUNDAMENTAL ATTRIBUTION ERROR—
THE CONFUSION OF CHARACTER AND SITUATION

A major insight of social psychology is the fundamental attribution error, which claims that people are too quick to understand the causes of other people's behavior in terms of internal character traits or dispositions and too slow to understand behavior in terms of external, situational causes. People more readily understand their own behavior in terms of situations, but less so the behavior of others. We are too quick to think that librarians are meticulous and lecturers talkative, without noticing that their jobs require them to be meticulous or talkative. We too quickly form strong first impressions of people without reflecting upon situational explanations of their behavior. We believe that our son-in-law is "a rather nervous type" without realizing that being around his in-laws makes him nervous. It appears that we give characterological explanations automatically, and only secondarily, if at all, consider the effect of context. This is arguably the biggest mistake people make in perceiving others.[14]

The fundamental attribution error can be usefully applied to pornography. One can view pornographic images as reflecting some characterological features of male sexuality that exist "inside" men's psyches, and claim, as John Stoltenberg incisively does, that pornography "tells lies about women, but . . . the truth about men."[15] No doubt pornography does tell lies about women and *a* truth about men. But is this truth merely a function of some preexistent sexist sexuality in men, or is it also a function of the *situation* of masturbation and of men's prior experience of stolen and intrusive images? I think the latter are insufficiently addressed in discussions of pornography.

In chapter 2 I discussed the finding that hits to self-esteem lead people to glorify their ingroup and denigrate out-groups. As I have implied, the impulse to masturbate is itself felt as painful to men's self-esteem, particularly to adolescents and postadolescents. Thus, images of pornography can be usefully seen as invitations for men to BIRG (bask in the reflected glory of) the image of masculinity that the gaze and pose of the pornographic model is intended to create in the male viewer. Men see themselves being seen as certain kinds of (often glorious) men in pornographic images. And they see themselves as failed men in the act of masturbating. The two go together. The impulse and context of masturbation lower men's self-esteem, and the content of the pornographic images encourages BIRGing in response to the lowered self-esteem. I do not want to minimize men's characterological sexism—it is all too prevalent. But the extreme sexism of much pornography must, in part, be seen in the context of masturbation.

In a larger context, the experience of stealing images and intrusive images is felt as injurious to self-esteem by men. This can only feed the BIRGing engaged in when using pornography—and the sexism of pornography.

FACE-ISM

Two findings about the effects of the relative prominence of faces presented in photos and pictures suggest that pornography may hurt women in unexpected ways.

First, in a study by Dane Archer of 1,750 photos and drawings found in *Time, Newsweek,* and other mainstream American media, men's faces were found to be given greater prominence than women's. That is, the male face took up a greater percentage of the picture or drawing. This finding was replicated in analyses of 3,500 photos published in eleven countries, in classic portraits of the seventeenth century, and the amateur drawings of college students. It has also shown up in women's magazines.[16]

This finding might seem innocent enough, but a second finding gives it greater meaning. When people are asked to evaluate strangers from photographs, those pictured with high facial prominence are perceived to be not only smarter, but more active, aggressive, and ambitious, regardless of their gender.[17]

This suggests that images of women that foreground their bodies serve as subtle propaganda encouraging us, well below the level of consciousness, to see women as less intelligent, active, aggressive, and ambitious than men. It is reasonable to infer that this is an effect of pornography.

PORNOGRAPHY AND THE FEAR
OF IDENTIFICATION WITH WOMEN

A further motive in the subjectification of women's bodies is to offer men arousal and gratification while minimizing men's risk of identifying with women. I have suggested that pornography seeks to offer men sexual arousal and gratification without risk to the self and that men's social perception of women's bodies—whether authorized, stolen, or intrusive—involves risk, as does the act of masturbation itself. In the partial service of reducing risk, pornography offers not images of whole, erotic, autonomous women, but rather subjectified bodies of women, that is, bodies whose putative consciousness and subjectivity, as manifest through facial expression and body posture, refer, and are a complement to, their viewability as bodies to be fantasized about by men. I want to comprehend men's need for dominative sex through a look at certain features of the experience of sexual arousal and sexual relating itself. To do this I will return to the psychoanalytic feminist work of Dorothy Dinnerstein and Nancy Chodorow.[18]

The experience of sexual arousal and "having sex with another" necessarily involves a loosening of identity boundaries. As I have suggested in chapter 2, predominantly mother-raised men get their often tenuously held identity as masculine by slowly separating from a mother with whom they were nearly psychically inseparable in early infancy, and identifying with a remote father and rather grandiose cultural stereotypes of masculinity. This shift in identification leaves some men perpetually uncertain of their masculinity and in possession of an insatiable need to prove it. Having sex with a woman threatens men's masculinity by unconsciously signaling a desire to regress and experience a certain infantile safety and union that was felt in the arms of mother. Hence, men defend themselves against this desire by relating to sex as an occasion for domination. Pornography can be seen as a kind of training in the emotion work of achieving arousal and gratification with minimal identification with women.

How does this process work? First, a look at arousal and sexual relating: Generally speaking, sexual arousal involves a lessening of self-consciousness and ego control, and regressively allowing biological processes to run their course. Sexual desire loosens identity boundaries for several reasons. It causes one to focus on spontaneous, somewhat involuntary, physical sensations and excitations rather than identifying with one's thoughts (the more one focuses on physical sensations instead of thoughts, the looser one's ego boundaries); sexual arousal relaxes muscular tensings and holdings that give one a felt sense of control over body image and one's ongoing background sense of identity; one's facial expression is more fluid and out of control—altering one's facial expression actively alters self-image.

If sexual arousal itself loosens ego boundaries, having sex with another person further intensifies the process. Mutual sexual desire usually involves instantaneous patterns of recognition of desire. I am aroused at my recognition of your arousal at your recognition of my arousal at my recognition of your arousal. And so on. My desire and your desire respond to and feed each other with such instantaneous automaticity that they may seem to fuse. Part of the meaning of one's own desire is to seek recognition of itself through arousing the other's desire through recognizing one's own desire.

Whatever the sources of such structural fusings in sex, they are intensified by the simple experience of being held. The more two lovers are focused and attuned to physical sensations of comfort and pleasure, and the less identified with thoughts, the greater the likelihood that they will feel fused and part of some larger, autonomous biological process. And the melting sensation of orgasm can further loosen one's boundaries—to say nothing of the experience of fusing as one's penis enters the vagina.

I want to explore some intuitions as to why the experience of having sex with women might threaten some men's sense of themselves as masculine and would cause them to defend against this by viewing sex as an occasion for domination. I have said that men are "sitting on" a problematic original identification with their mothers and that they are prone to create and conquer stress, or relate to preexistent distress, as a way of separating themselves from their mothers and feeling superior to women. Virtually any kind of distress can be an occasion to "take it like a man" and prove manhood.

But the experience of having sex with a woman offers the greatest potential threat of all to manhood. Being held by a woman threatens many men with a deeply repressed desire to return to the safety of their mother's arms. Such a desire is felt as threatening because it might entail a loss of the sense of the self as masculine and potentially as an appearance of homoerotic desires. (If I am identified with mother, I may become attracted to father. See chapter 6.) It should be easy to see how sex becomes an occasion for men to prove masculinity through "dominative fucking." Sex becomes something a man does to a woman. Our most fundamental conception of sex, as manifest through linguistic usage, views sex as an act of aggressive degradation done by a man to a woman: "I want to fuck her."

Men's need to be in control of sexual feeling is in part a need to control a repressed desire to identify with women. Pornography can thus be seen, in light of all of the above, as a means of achieving arousal and gratification without risking identification with women. Being aroused by looking at what one can control—an image held in the hand—is safe for men, especially if the image is tailored to cushion and bolster men's egos. Looking distances men from women; the stereotyped images of pornography further distance and defamiliarize women from men.

And there is a way men have sex with women as if their partner's body is a pornographic image. They fuck the image of the body more than the body itself. The body becomes something more seen than felt. The visual supersedes the tactile. The tactile, with its greater threat of identification, is diminished. And the use of sexually exciting images during sex can offer a man a kind of safety against the threat of identification. What might pornography look like if men felt freer to meld and identify with women during sex or if women and sex were not so often an occasion to prove masculinity through a dominating phallic athleticism? It is impossible to describe what does not yet exist. I will only say that pornography would be less worshipful of the penis and more respectful of women.

Heterosexual men may deeply fear identification with women because they unconsciously desire it. But they also badly need nurturance and sex from women. And, for many men, to have both nurturance and sex at the same time is too threatening. One way to cope with this is to divide women into Madonnas and whores; the Madonna offers nurturance and the whore offers sex—but only at a safe psychic distance. It is as if women offering both sex and nurturance might overwhelm men's sense of their own masculinity—might pull them back across the divide they crossed in early infancy that brought them to manhood. Too much satisfaction of psychic need might overwhelm their masculine defenses.

Both views of women are important in struggling to think politically about pornography.

MADONNA SEXISTS AND WHORE SEXISTS, SEX AS PLEASURE AND SEX AS RELATING

The attempt to arrive at a politics of pornography has divided the world of feminist women. It divides me as well. Pornography is like a prism attracting and diffracting the light generated by competing, often implicit, models of sex and forms of sexism. What one sees when one looks at pornography tends to be a function of the light generated by implicit, sometimes unconscious assumptions about sex and sexism. Sexual conservatives decry pornography because it is wildly sexual, feminists attack it because it is perniciously sexist, advocates of sexual freedom celebrate its open sexuality, and still other feminists acknowledge its sexism but seek to honor its potential to help liberate women's sexuality. I aspire not so much to a finely polished coherent position (a "foolish consistency") as to present some of my own struggles to think about pornography.

I want to roughly delineate two conceptions of sex and two kinds of sexism. The two conceptions of sex are the human relating model and the intensity of pleasure model. Two kinds of sexism are whore sexism and Madonna sexism. These distinctions are meant as fluid, provisional aids to thought, identifiable methods by which pornography can be, in fact is, understood. I want to first explain these models, show something about how they "interact," and then apply them more concretely to pornography.

The human relating model views sex as a form of communication, an expression of affection and love, and (in its traditional form) as heterosexual and sanctified by matrimony. Sex is sacred, beautiful, dignified, pure, clean, tender, and gentle. Sexual pleasure is an intimate gift offered to the beloved. The relating model represents the proper view of sex associated with the mainstream America of the 1950s and is advocated by many sexual conservatives today.

The intensity of pleasure model legitimates sheer pleasure

as a motivation for sex. Varieties of partners, the absence of requisite intimacy, the exploration of technique, the presentation of self and perception of others as potential sources of sexual pleasure, and the tolerance of diverse desire are all part of the pleasure model. The pleasure model has most purely manifested itself in parts of the pre-AIDS gay subculture. The pleasure model has evolved among heterosexuals over the last thirty years as a response to the putative hypocrisy, repressiveness, and intolerance of the relating model and to the increased availability and effectiveness of birth control, which has freed women to explore pleasure sex. The advent of AIDS has encouraged a return to viewing sex as relating. Pleasure sex and relating sex exist as historical and psychological complements. Generally speaking, proponents and practitioners of pleasure sex tolerate proponents of relating sex better than the converse. Pleasure sex is sometimes presented as a complement to relating sex; conservative Christians like Marabel Morgan have encouraged wives to learn to give their husbands intense pleasure in the service of God and Marriage.[19]

Whore and Madonna sexism reflect tendencies to relate to women as either degraded objects of lust or as nurturant, "pure" mothers and wives. Whore sexism expresses male lust as a kind of revenge against women's capacity to arouse. Whore-sexist men may have great difficulty honoring women's subjectivity and autonomy. Rape is the most egregious expression of whore sexism. In its extreme versions, all sex with the Madonna is rape; forced sex can never be rape with

the whore. Whore sexism is always denigrating but not always lusting; a man or woman might engage in whore
sexism by denigrating a sexually expressive woman without
lusting after her. Madonna sexism exalts woman's domestic
role as nurturer and sentimentalizes the soft, gentle, and
fragile feminine. Madonna sexism tends to view women as
too soft to engage with the harsh, unsentimental realities of
life; hence women function best in the safety of the home.
Madonna sexism denies and would repress the reality, complexity and earthiness of women's lust. Whore sexism and
Madonna sexism coexist strongly in many men, who would
be glad to see "the bitch wiggling her ass in a miniskirt get
raped" (whore sexism) while feeling ready to kill anybody
who touched their wives or sisters (Madonna sexism). Men
or women may be more overtly whore or Madonna sexist,
but it is impossible to be one without implicitly supporting
the other. Whore sexism and Madonna sexism uphold and
imply each other. They define women with the same categories, sexuality and nurturance, while judging the Madonna as up and the whore down. The whore has wildly sexual things done to her and can experience sexual pleasure;
she is not nurturant. Men are not allowed to touch the
Madonna, who is the essence of nurturance. Both conceptions view women as primarily passive and victimized; both
distance and defamiliarize women from men. Both view
women in terms of men's power over them. Any conception
of women that distances women from men and makes it
difficult for men to relate to women's experience is sexist and

oppressive to women. Whore sexism and Madonna sexism both seek to destroy women's sexuality: whore sexism by making sexual freedom and expression unsafe for women through sexual abuse and denigration; Madonna sexism by denying the varieties of possible sexual expression in women. Words such as "slut," "cunt," and "piece of ass" are whore sexist; words like "womanhood," "femininity," and "virtuous woman," when used prescriptively, are Madonna sexist.

The pleasure model of sex tends to encourage whore sexism in men because many men cannot find a woman sexy without wanting to degrade her sexiness. The relating model of sex tends to encourage, and be associated with, Madonna sexism, and vice versa. Both minimize the association of woman and pleasure. Pleasure sex is only morally defensible if people possess the willingness and ability to acknowledge and respect each other's "humanity." Given men's historical difficulty at respecting women, pleasure sex is morally problematic.

On the other hand, a woman experimenting with pleasure sex may be striking a blow against Madonna sexism. The threat of whore sexism (sexual abuse or denigration for being sexual) can move a woman away from pleasure sex toward relating sex.

Men and women who actively oppose whore sexism—for example, through antirape work or through opposing the whore sexism of pornography—run the risk of supporting Madonna sexism. In opposing sexual domination and objectification and rape, in struggling to be respectful of women, it is easy to fall into traditional Madonna-sexist modes of respectfulness and sentimentality: Since women aren't really whores and sex objects to be fucked, they must really be Madonnas who want sex to be nurturant, loving, and communicative, or who don't want sex at all. It is a mistake to allow rapists and whore sexists to define what sex ought or ought not to be between consenting antisexist men and women; to do so gives them more power than they deserve. There is nothing *inherently* sexist about a man wanting to do things to a woman's body as long as such desires are balanced with a strongly enacted respect for, and acknowledgment of, women.

To apply the above-discussed models of sex and sexism to pornography, I have chosen an example that is somewhat atypical but helps highlight some ambiguities of pornography. A *Penthouse* centerfold spoke with pride of her work as a stripper, describing herself as slowly, artfully arousing her mostly male audience and herself, taking them "as far as they could go" and herself "as far as she could go." When they could "stand it no longer," she walked off the stage.

Consider seven views of this pornographic performance.

1. A man or woman involved in pleasure sex might approve because they find it is arousing.
2. A sexual conservative who views sex as relating might disapprove because it does not show sex as relational and misvalues sex and its appropriate place in human life.

3. An antipornography feminist might disapprove because it encourages men in whore sexism and is thus whore sexist itself.

4. A whore-sexist man might approve because it makes him feel superior to and sexual toward women. He might regard the stripper as a "nice piece of ass."

5. An antipornography Madonna sexist might disapprove because it assaults the honor and dignity of womanhood, that is, it threatens his or her Madonna sexism.

6. A pro-pornography feminist might approve because it shows a woman being sexual and powerful and thus strikes a blow against Madonna sexism.

7. A Madonna-sexist man, resisting his sexual attraction to the stripper through whore sexism that is denigrating but not lusting, might disapprovingly regard her as a whore.

The example is atypical in that most strippers may not feel much pride and power in their work; it would probably be difficult for most feminists to see many strippers as striking a blow against Madonna sexism. But the example is useful in revealing the range of responses to pornography. For most of us, competing models of sex and sexism live in our psyches and compete for attention as emotional responses when we contemplate pornography. Emotional responses always involve and presuppose, in fact *are* in part, evaluations of the world. It is both useful and necessary to identify the cognitive sources of such evaluations. Otherwise much confusion can ensue.

For example, the religious right has opposed pornography, in part because it threatens Madonna sexism; that is, because it degrades *femininity* or *womanhood,* two Madonna-sexist notions of women. Feminists have opposed pornography for its whore sexism, because it degrades *women.* There is a world of difference between being against pornography because it is whore sexist and being against it because it affronts one's own Madonna sexism.

One of the reasons I find pornography difficult to assess is because it is genuinely possible for a pornographic image, film, or performance to encourage, or at least be an occasion for, whore sexism and militate against Madonna sexism at the same time. The stripper described above is encouraging men to view her as an object of lust; to encourage lust is to encourage whore sexism in some men. Yet in being erotically wild and proud and powerful she is legitimating a part of women's sexuality that Madonna sexism would repress. Pornography can be a force against Madonna sexism (and by implication whore sexism) when the woman appears to be proud, erotically powerful, and authentically human.

Any "sexy" image of a woman, even if the content of the image is not whore sexist, will be related to by many men in a whore-sexist manner. And any image of a sexy woman that is sold, no matter what the content, will encourage men to view women and sexual pleasure as commodities to be bought, sold, gotten for free, or stolen—that is, raped. But the fact that many men don't respect women ought not to keep other men and women from exploring their sexuality through nonsexist images.

Another source of confusion: to say that the dissemination of an image is sexist or objectionable is not to say that the practice depicted is sexist or objectionable. For example, in a society with many men who massively disrespect women, we do not need images disseminated of women bound and gagged, because such images are likely to legitimate such disrespect. On the other hand, a woman exploring her sexuality, playing with being tied up, may be doing something anti–Madonna sexist. We ought to discourage disrespect for women in images, yet free women and men in consensual practices.

It is a mistake to view all sexuality as a manifestation of men's oppression of women. Gender does not "own" sexuality—sexuality is a child that, to a degree, can talk, walk, indeed strut, by itself. It has a life, history, hierarchies, and modes of legitimation all its own. People, independent of gender, are oppressed by the fact of their sexual practices. Men's oppression of women can cause us to perceive sexuality as an unattractive sideproduct of gender. A man on top of a woman, powerfully thrusting into her vagina, is not necessarily reproducing men's oppression of women. A woman getting excited by feigning resistance with her lover and being overcome is not necessarily reflecting some "internalized oppression" as a woman. It is (to repeat) a mistake to allow rapists and other oppressive men to define the appropriateness of our sexual pleasures. Sexual pleasure, like the pleasures of eating, may just be various, shifting, idiosyncratic, eccentric, and not necessarily psychologically or sociologically motivated. Because the "content" and "effect" of sexual pleasure will always in part be psychological does not mean that the *motivation* for what *gives pleasure* must be.

Having stated all the above I want to reiterate a point made earlier. Most of what I see in the magazines in pornography stores strikes me as whore sexist, that is, disrespectful of women and vengeful toward women's capacity to arouse. Whatever pornography's potential to help free us, it is not being realized.

SEXISM AND SEXUAL REPRESSION

As Michael Kimmel has argued, the two great forces that inform pornography are sexism and sexual repression.[20] We need an overriding theoretical orientation that encompasses them and gives us the tools with which to understand their relation. Such an analysis is beyond the scope of this book; here, I will simply offer a few observations.

Harry Brod makes the point that the process of men grading women's attractiveness is a way men distance themselves from their sexuality. It is a way of "evading their own subjectivity in terms of public sanction of their desires."[21] Grading is a way of bonding with other men while keeping one's desires from overwhelming one. One can say that the sexist act of objectifying is also an act of repression. Or is it that the sexism is a response to greater sexual freedom for women? Is sexism related to a form of repression required by sexual freedom? Eli Sagan argues that the freeing of sexuality brings with it great fear in men and a need to repress women's sexuality out of fear of losing manhood.[22]

The splitting of women into Madonna and whores is a way of separating one's own lust from affection; and it is a form of sexist oppression that seeks to repress the lust of women one loves or might love. It appears that the men who are most afraid of their own lust must repress the lust of women they love or respect. One can point to a certain circle: men bond out of a fear of women and women's sexuality; that bonding necessitates the separation of sex and affection—if they go together then affection between men becomes sexually threatening; the separation of sex and affection makes men more sexist. Such a circle shows sexual repression and sexism supporting each other.

Finally, men's heterosexual lust must be decontaminated from gender and the need to prove manhood. As Lynne Segal puts it:

> For those of us who want to see the recognition of women's equality and agency in every sphere of life, [hetero]'sexuality' as confirmation of 'manhood' is an idea we must attack. . . . In the meantime, we can continue to insist, with all the passion we can muster, that

there is no necessary fit between maleness, activity and desire; any more than there is a fit between femaleness, passivity and sexual responsiveness.[23]

If sex could be denuded of the need to prove manhood, men would let out a loud but secret sigh that would change the weather. And gays would feel a lightening of oppression—if straight sex did not prove manhood, gay sex would not disprove it. Straight men's sexuality has had a rough time of it lately. Women's sexuality has been ennobled, spiritualized, and reenchanted by feminists. It would be wonderful if male heterosexuality, freed of its vengeful degradation of women and contorting quest for manhood, could reenchant itself.

4

Reflections on Mothers,
Grief, and Sexism

A not admitting of the wound
Until it grew so wide
That all my Life had entered it
And there were troughs beside.
Emily Dickinson

I want to shift tones and return to the personal. I have
spoken in a theoretical way about the importance of men's
relations to their mothers in understanding compulsive
masculinity, men's fear of identification with women, and
sexism. The reader may legitimately ask: What of the author's relationship with his mother? How does it fit the theorizing in the last two chapters? How strongly grounded is the
theory in his own experience?

I am drawn to certain intuitions about men and their
mothers. The resonance of these intuitions in my own experience is murky and elusive, but nonetheless real and, at
moments, powerful. I can only capture that resonance in-
completely, by approaching the issue haltingly and from

different angles. I only have small parts of the puzzle in place, and it is a trial to put it together and nearly impossible to see the whole.

I begin with some reflections that center around my mother's death.

· · · · ·

Mother:
Since your death thirty years ago, your presence is a film covering my experience, darkening it and making the world, the world of my life, seem farther away. If I could pop you open, a thousand memories would appear and move me, breaking and healing my heart, and making the world real again. Your unreality places the world so far away. Your unreality makes my life unreal. But I can't, don't know how to pop you open, and as I move deeper into middle age, I wonder whether the attention I give you is worth the effort. But still, I sense, until you are real, I will not be real.

Or so it seems when I think of my mother. She died when I was thirteen, quickly, in agony, of cancer. She was told it was a slipped disc. I think I was in love with her. By the time she died I had lived in twelve houses in nine cities. I barely knew anyone outside my nuclear family and was, owing to his erratic violence, terrified of my father. She was *it*.

I remember the day she died. My father put his arms around my brother and me and said, "The doctors don't think your mother is going to make it through the day."

(I sob as I write this, but my sobbing feels as much like a physical convulsion as an emotion; as much like a cough as a cry; maybe a third of the emotional meaning is in it. My body sobs at the thought of her death—my psyche denies most of the meaning. Sobbing with much of the passion missing: This is the ongoing story of my grief; my body wants to grieve but something in me resists. As if, over time, my soul is trying to reenter my body. Over the years my tears for her have never felt quite real. Maybe we—men—need new words to register the varying degrees of feeling and meaning present in a cry.)

The three of us wept. That night at the hospital, she lay howling in pain, making gurgling noises. My brother and I sat on either side of the bed crying. She was mostly bones by then. In four months she must have gone from 140 pounds to 60. I doubt that it is possible for a person to be any bonier. She howled. Leaving, we kissed her on the cheek and for the first time she gave no sign of recognition. Her mind had been going for the last couple of weeks.

My father told us we would remember Mommy as she was, with a clear head.

I remember going to sleep that night. My father came and woke me up.

"Mommy's in heaven. She's gone."

I felt a sense of relief that it was over. I remember crying. I remember some faint image of heaven. And I remember something else. I went into the bathroom and stared into the mirror and, smiling angrily through my tears, thought to myself, "I'm not going to let this get to me."

I think I had been playing with my emotions for years.

At the funeral I stared and stared and stared at her as if I were trying to stare her down. I liked it. I was in some altered, trance-like state. I stared a long time and then was led away by the funeral director, as if I needed looking after. I resented this. I was fine and wanted to stare some more. Maybe I was trying to cultivate some cold-bloodedness; maybe this was an expression of rage. Maybe I was trying to protect myself from overwhelming grief. I imagine the funeral director thought I was showing signs of shock. Or maybe I was becoming an embarrassment.

Afterward I was angry at God and decided he must not exist if he could allow this. The problem of reconciling evil with God troubled me.

After she died, my father, my brother (Richard, who was sixteen), and I did not talk about her. *Did not talk about her.* Or almost never. Our grief was private, for the most part.

Once my father came to me in tears.

"Why did this have to happen to us? You and Rich have your school, but you are all I have."

I remember his face when they closed the coffin for the

last time; I remember how he fought with his tears as he walked back to sit down with us.

Another time he came to me:

"You know your mother was one of the smartest people who ever lived. You could come to her with a problem, and she would help you talk about it and work it through."

My father hated his mother; he addressed my mother as mommy. A letter he wrote to her in 1953 begins, "Dearest Mommy," and ends with him saying what a great mommy she is. Despite the cold, terrifying anger he was capable of, he could be wonderfully tender. I still cherish the way he would tuck me in as a child and tell me that he loved me with the dearest sweet talk.

We were three men living on an army post in the deep South in 1964, with tanks stored four hundred yards away. We did not know how to comfort each other, or how to grieve, or how to vivify her memory. She had been the emotional center of our lives. None of us had enduring sources of emotional support apart from her.

When someone close to us dies, we are left with a hole in our lives. Ideally, as we grieve, we slowly acknowledge what we have lost, and the hole is filled with the memories of the person, with warm feelings of love, with a recognition of how the person lives on in ourselves and the world. The void becomes rich and fertile as the deceased becomes a source of energy and strength. Nothing like that happened when my mother died.

I cried a lot for some time. And, because of that, I assumed that I had properly grieved for my mother. But as I got much older, in my thirties, I slowly came to recognize that I had not.

It is sometimes said that unresolved grief is at the core of depression. I have, in varying degrees, been depressed much, maybe most of my life, in ways recognizable to those close to me. What is the connection?

My mother is a presence who comes and goes. I have intuitions, intimations of her presence, her meaning in my life, but for the most part she is mystified. I am forty-three. I have begun to feel that by the time I die I may understand her effect on me. It is very slow going. In writing this I want to speed her up. One's childhood, as it appears before one has a deceptive look of truth, as if one's reconstituted memories were one's true life as a child. But I step back from the picture and remind myself that I remember but a tiny fraction of my life as a child, and that the picture I possess of my childhood—and my mother—is but one picture, that forms and reforms itself, and not my true childhood, not her.

She manifests herself in so many ways.

A running joke for several years is this. When someone does something I mildly disapprove of, I say, "If you think you are hurting *anyone* but yourself, you are *very, sadly* mistaken." This usually gets a laugh.

When I say this I am saying something my mother said to me many times. I am simultaneously assuming her identity and power and mocking it. And I am using her to get a laugh.

Sometimes I reflect upon the women I have been involved with and I think, "They are all *one* woman; all one woman underneath. At my deepest center I do not discriminate, do not notice who is there at my side. At my deepest center is one woman I am responding to, tailoring my personality to, entertaining, impressing, charming—my mother."

We were very affectionate, my mother and I. We kissed a lot; she hugged me often. I was physically precocious, five foot seven inches and shaving at twelve, the first in gym class to have pubic hair. And lust ridden at an early age and unable somehow to masturbate to orgasm. In our own way, my mother and I possessed some physical connection I do not understand. I have said this since I was about twenty. I am not entirely sure what I mean.

Exactly a month before she died, she came home for a night. I remember ministering to her. She could not walk by then. I remember getting her a pitcher so she could urinate as she lay in bed. When I placed it near her genitals, I was jolted by a vivid glimpse of her vagina. I felt a powerful, confused thrill. I had not looked head on at a woman's vagina in this way before. I felt like I was seeing something I was not supposed to see.

At my father's funeral I was surrounded by relatives I had mostly not seen since my mother's funeral some twenty years before. A first cousin of my father's said he was struck by how much my facial expression resembled my mother's. I have no idea what he was talking about and probably never will. The thought that I wear her on my face, in my facial expressions and manner, is both terrifying and comforting.

For a long time I would cry at evocations of goodness. I remember seeing a segment of "60 Minutes" about a couple who had adopted some fifteen "problem" children and, apparently, through giving them love, had enabled them to adjust to life in a family. I cried when I saw this without knowing why. Once when I was twenty-three I played the last five minutes of *The Wizard of Oz* over and over and cried at Dorothy's line, "There's no place like home!" Watching Clinton's inauguration ceremonies, I sobbed when Marilyn Horne sang the Shaker song ("'Tis a gift to be simple, 'tis a gift to be free") and a song about children of different colors ("Make a rainbow, make a rainbow"). I taped this and would return to it and cry again and again. For a long time I had little idea why I was crying. Then, slowly, over the years, I came to believe that it had something to do with my mother. But what was the connection?

I came across these words in a book on romantic love by Stephen Goldbart and David Wallin: "Becoming aware of the goodness of love in the present can, unexpectedly, trigger grief. . . . we may grieve for what we have had and lost. Or we may grieve for what the past has never given us." [1]

This told me what I knew but hadn't quite thought. My

mother's goodness, her affection and kindness and good-will, which gave me joy and safety—however romanti-cized—is gone and will not come back. But I carry it inside me somewhere, and the presence of human kindness awak-ens my simultaneous longing for it and grief at its absence.

She was buried some seventy miles south of us, in Nash-ville, Tennessee. I remember on cold rainy nights wondering what it must be like out there, in a box in the rain. When I was twenty-two, I wrote a fragmentary poem about it.

Your Mother Wears Combat Boots!

my mother wears no shoes
she's in a box
outside
in the rain
in the rain
in a box
she wears no shoes, hears no views, sings no blues
in the rain
in the box
underground
not a sound
does reach her
not a sound
goes round
in her head
or her toes

no one knows what it's like in a box in the rain
with no shoes

it's insane what that box could contain
just insane

.   .   .   .   .

A question arises: I say that making my mother—the memory of my mother—come alive will make me come alive, make the world real to me. And I find myself drawn to the intuition that men are sitting on and fighting some deep, troubled, residual identification with their mothers in the name of their manhood. Is my theorizing a projection of my own psychic needs and condition? Do I see men in this light because of my desire to brighten my own reality by reclaiming the buried mother inside me whose death left me incomplete? It is a reasonable question I am unsure how to answer. The mother that men fight off is the internalized preoedipal mother, the mother who dominates and *is* one's world before one acquires gender—the mother whose existence is alive in men at a preverbal level. The mother who existed prior to the ordering effects of language on experience, when everything existed at a level of irretrievable intensity. The mother I long for is the pre-oedipal mother, but also an older mother who represented safety in the presence of a frightening father.

Dorothy Dinnerstein, more than anyone, in *The Mermaid and the Minotaur,* has brought alive the pre-oedipal mother and her profound effects on the lives and psyches of both men and women. Dinnerstein calls for something terrifying as a part of the end of sexism: mother—the romanticized mother of motherhood and apple pie, pure and innocent and loving—must die. She may only have existed in our fantasies, and her image is born of guilt at our rage toward her, but to move on, we must let go of her. It seems clear enough that the entry of women into the paid work force is putting an end to her and turning motherhood, in Jessica Benjamin's words, into a "disenchanted symbol." It is no accident that those men who most romanticize and sentimentalize motherhood are also quickest to devalue the role of mothering and its legitimacy as work.

· · · · ·

Is seems to me that, for men, the capacity to grieve is tied to the capacity to empathize with women. Grief is a form of self-nurturance; it is deeply humbling, a form of acknowledgment of that which has been beautiful in life and is now gone. Proving manhood often annihilates the capacity to grieve. Too many men cannot be humbled without feeling humiliated.

In *The Crossing Guard,* Jack Nicholson plays a man who has lost his daughter to a drunk driver. He is unable to nurture and refresh himself through grief and instead obsesses about the man who killed her and is soon to get out of prison as the movie opens. We see Nicholson with his buddies at strip shows, full of grotesque, drunken laughter. These are men who are manifestly sexist and manifestly unable to grieve. As I have suggested, the earliest and most salient stress that boys, on their compulsive way to becoming men, endure and conquer is the impulse to cry, to grieve. Nothing in my experience hurts like convulsing in grief, but it is an alive hurt and, potentially, a restorative one. Perhaps the original grief is the loss of the safety of mother, who assuaged the hourly griefs of babyhood. This is a grief that is unacknowledged, repressed, and awakened by subsequent grief.

I have experienced a certain momentary awe, always tinged with fear, before certain women's knowledge of my emotions, a feeling that they can see into parts of me that I cannot see. I think this awe carries echoes of the time when my mother understood my needs better than I could. It is a terrifying awe: I am terrified of needs to be mothered that, if gratified, would leave me in a state of intolerable vulnerability. Because the time of mother's greatest power has its origins in infancy, before the onset of language, the awakening of deep feelings about one's mother is blurry and confused, and the achievement of manhood leaves them further repressed and difficult to identify.

I am told, and I dimly remember, that I called my mother's breasts "dodors." Apparently, at a young age while my parents were entertaining, I walked into the living room and began tugging at my mother's blouse, saying, "I want my dodors!" I am charmed by this. Even now, sucking on a bottle that allows one to really suck brings me back to some state I long for; this is one entree into imagining the state of identification with my mother. And I have had spontaneous experiences of curling up in the fetal position and wanting to rock away into some blissful eternity. I all too easily can imagine dissolving in maternal identification. *But,* if I experience a woman I am close to as overbearing, I readily protest and withdraw and feel threatened.

And, as I suggested in chapter 2, it isn't really someone I know as mother I want to meld with, but the "pregendered mother" who existed before I had a knowledge of gender. One way of stating the problem is this: when boys discover that they are boys and that their mother is a woman, they know that they are in trouble. That mothers turn out to be women and boys turn out to be boys is deeply unfortunate, and finally unnecessary. For "boys" and "women" are cultural, not biological concepts; they embody notions of what certain-sexed humans should be.

One form of sexism that connects to my mother is this. I am less tolerant of insensitive women than of insensitive men; I expect more empathy and simple human understanding from women. This is "idealizing sexism"—I see women as, in certain respects, better than men and punish them when they are not. There is a feminist or pseudofeminist side to this: I have bashed men and seen women as superior. But maybe I am just imposing on women the task of nurturing that I expected from my mother.

I grapple with a contradiction. As a male, boys feel superior to girls and wander off in grandiose fantasies of maleness, yet mothers retain enormous psychic power over sons; they were experienced as virtually omniscient and omnipotent at one time. From one perspective, proving manhood is an effort to disempower mothers by doing what she is too "feminine" to do. In my case it took many forms.

Learning to swear was something I was late in getting to. I cried easily as a child and struggled often to hold back tears. Tears around other boys were a source of shame; they evoked the terror of losing all the social esteem—the manhood that I had worked so hard to achieve—in one gush of release. Yet, tears around my mother brought comfort that I cherished. Learning to swear was a flight from pain into anger for me, the opposite of a good cry. If crying always echoes crying out for the mother, swearing is a toughening that draws boys away from her and toward some ideal of masculinity. Swearing creates its own scar tissue. During the summer of my eleventh year, older boys taught me "bitch" and "bastard," "fuck" and "shit" and "fart," "motherfucker" and "cocksucker," and other words it was necessary to know how to use to be a man. I energetically took up swearing. Learning to swear was a way of renouncing being a goody-goody momma's boy and, by implication, a way of learning sexism. It encouraged a kind of Madonna sexism: most women were assumed to be too weak to swear and one watched one's words around them. And the swear words themselves included sexist ones that degraded women, which, so far as I can recall, I mostly tended to resist, although the taboo language of sex was full of sexism. And "bitch," arguably an essentially sexist word, and clearly a word easily used in a sexist way, came readily from my lips.

I had entered a realm of masculine toughness through swearing. My mother would have been shocked to know that I used such words; she never went farther than "darn." "Damn" was the great taboo-breaker in my family.

I remember playing baseball with my mother watching; my ability to do what she could not do, and her recognition of this, disempowered her in my mind. I was a man, something she could never be. Through this process I began to confuse admiration with love. Being affirmed as a man by my mother meant being admired as superior to her. Wanting to be admired as superior has lingered on in my relations with women in ways that have subtly deprived me of love. It is a subtle form of sexism that has diminished over time.

5

The Sports Page

The loneliest thing I know
Is my own mind at play.
Theodore Roethke

Proving manhood, in its purer forms, is perhaps most visible in sports. My own daily engagement with the sports page is a vantage point from which to explore this.

First, a caveat: proving manhood in no way exhausts the meaning and reality of sports for men. There is much that is good about sports: the animal delight in the full engagement of one's body and senses in an activity; the aesthetic delight of watching sports; the moral value of an activity in which performance counts most and where the outcome is just; the social pleasure of acting as part of a coordinated group; the pleasure of energized desire when we care deeply about winning or losing; the pleasure for adults of retaining a continuity with one's childhood; and much more. But sports is sufficiently embroiled with the grandiosity and sexism found in compulsive masculinity to merit exploration.

．　．　．　．　．

Call it an addiction if you wish—I have been stuck on the sports page since I was five years old. It has become an alienated pleasure that falls somewhere between an affliction and an affection. The sports page offers a zone of fantasy and brain chemistry so much a part of me that it seems more like something that happens to me than something I do. McLuhan remarked that people don't read the morning paper, they get into it like a warm bath. I don't read the sports page, I sit and watch it unfold before and around me. The sports page has been for me a realm of deeply ambivalent magic, identification, glory, grieving, community, desperation, moral engagement, and God-knows-what, all happening in breakneck mystification. It is suffused with infantile meaning in a way I hanker to grasp. It also involves the pursuit of identity in a form I consciously disavow through irony and silence.

I have taken one morning's sports page and tried to record the flips and turns of my unfolding consciousness; and I have attempted to make sense of what goes on as I read it and to discern some implications for men and women. I deliberately chose a Sunday morning in the middle of the baseball season. I read the paper sitting at the computer and wrote down what was happening to me as I read. Of course, perceived things change from being recorded, and my vigilant attention no doubt caused me to experience the sports page differently than I would have otherwise.

I was going out of my way to record the crazy hidden whispers of my mind.

· · · · ·

It is Sunday, July 11, 1993, the middle of the baseball season. After reading the front page and a few stories in the news section, I turn to the sports page. It is an agreeable feeling; the only place in the paper where I feel confident I am in for some pleasure. My eyes move to the headline about the Oakland A's baseball game—they have lost. A subhead says that Todd Van Poppel, a young A's pitcher who was regarded two years ago as the best eighteen-year-old in the country, will not be sent down to the minors despite his disastrous start last week—his first start in the majors. This draws my attention. Van Poppel has a great fastball but is just learning his other pitches. So much has been expected of him; the A's gambled to get him and won. He chose, contrary to expectations, to skip college and turn pro straight out of high school. I want him to blow everyone away. I skim the story of the A's loss and turn to the line score to see how people did; there is no one to identify with. Rickey Henderson did not play; if he had I would have gotten pleasure if he had stolen another base or hit a home run or even scored a run. He is possibly the best leadoff hitter in baseball history.

I start skimming the other line scores; I see that Will Clark of the Giants went 1 for 4. I am glad he is having a bad year. He has had a great career but he is a known racist and has a tough exterior I don't like. His eyes are harsh. I'm glad to see him screwing up.

I skim other box scores. I find Bo Jackson of the White Sox who went 0 for 2; I am glad they have been playing him lately, but bothered by the plummeting of his average down to 230. I feel a touch of depression seeing his box score. I am worried that he will strike out so often that his comeback will not be a success. He is arguably the greatest athlete who ever lived and I am deeply compelled by his superhuman abilities. I sometimes get a thrill thinking about him. Before his terrible hip injury in a football game, he was the fastest and strongest running back in professional football. He would remove his baseball uniform in October, take a week off, and step onto the football field and immediately make great runs. He is the stuff of movies, barely believable. And, as a baseball player, he was one of the fastest runners, strongest arms, and most powerful batters before his injury. Again, barely believable. He and Michael Jordan are the most superhuman figures in sports, and I am thrilled by them. When the *New York Times* published an article by a professor explaining that, contrary to appearances, Jordan does not actually break the laws of gravity when he leaps and appears to hang in the air, I got a big bang out of it.

I look around the sports page some more; Dwight Gooden of the Mets didn't pitch. I'm still bothered that Larry King said Darryl Strawberry is destined for the Hall of Fame and Gooden isn't. How ridiculous! I see that Saberhagen pitched. His name evokes a brief image of his wide-breaking curve ball; I have captured it in slow motion on my VCR. Curve balls are a source of magic to me—the more they break, the more magical. I could throw a wicked one when I was a kid. I would love to be an umpire behind the plate watching curve balls. What I feel toward them approaches religious awe—I am amazed at their very existence.

I check to see how Cecil Fielder did for the Tigers. He knocked in a run, which makes it 80 so far this year; I calculate that he will knock in around 140 and hit 44 home runs at this pace. Figures that make me feel foolishly powerful and secure. I occasionally assess how a player is doing by calculating what their final statistics will be if they continue at the present pace. I was good at mental arithmetic as a child, I think owing in part to my involvement with the sports page.

About once every three years I walk into a bookstore, find the sports section, study a book that has the career statistics of players, and experience a series of thrills. Last time I did it I was amazed at Joe DiMaggio's RBI production; I had never quite gotten his mystique until then. When I was seven and came across Ted Williams's baseball card, I went gaga over his numbers.

I am still searching for that gaga feeling. Sports statistics are incontrovertible. They cannot really be argued with. Certain numbers fill me with something—pride, awe, manhood, honor; they are mood elevators, rushes of energy.

Back to the page. I see that Valenzuela pitched a two-hitter and is continuing his comeback. He now has pitched twenty-three consecutive shutout innings. He's showing them he can still do it. I am glad—he has an innocent quality and I like the way he rolls his eyes when he pitches. Also he's a screwball pitcher, something unique that I respect.

I see the headline that the San Francisco Forty-Niners have no quarterback controversy and think of Steve Young, a good guy. I skim a sports news column that puts players' names in boldface. I see that basketball player David Wingate has signed a new contract and feel sad; he was so good as a college player, but, as a pro, he's just another no-name. I follow college players into the pros and feel depressed at their lackluster careers.

I go to the two columns of statistics covering hitting and pitching. A few years ago I would dwell on these statistics, checking how people were doing. These days I spend less time on it.

Now I skim it and occasionally calculate season home runs and RBIs based on current records. Looking for the few players I root for, I start at the bottom with the low averages and move up. The longer it takes me to find their names the better I feel because it means their averages will be higher. Over the years several have been sources of interest: Bo Jackson, Reggie Jackson, Jose Canseco, and Dave Winfield.

I look for Canseco—the poor fool is having an operation because he hurt his arm pitching an inning. He is normally an outfielder. I see he has 10 homers and 46 RBIs in 231 at bats; I quickly establish that for a full season he would have 25 homers and 115 RBIs, a little weak on homers for him but good on RBIs. His swing is a wonder to behold; I can instantly visualize the way he explodes when he hits the ball and the power he has. I continue to scan. Dave Winfield, although forty, is doing well. I tend to think of age in terms of baseball players—I am forty-three and not thrilled by it. Almost no one my age can play major league baseball except a few relief pitchers who throw knuckle balls. I also estimate distances by imagining hitting a baseball; short distances I imagine shooting a basketball.

Still moving up the column, I see that Olerud and Gallaraga are still hitting over 390 and feel a little sad because it's inevitable that they will crash before the end of the season. I wonder how Kevin Mitchell, formerly a great home run hitter, is doing. He has started to come back after not doing so well. Looking for him, I notice Deion Sanders, the closest thing to Bo Jackson around. He's only hitting 259, but he has 20 runs scored in 169 at bats and would have close to 80 in a year, at least respectable. Still looking for Mitchell, I find he's hitting 357. I had no idea. And with 15 home runs and 52 RBIs, he's definitely on the way back. Unfortunately, I have reason to believe he's an asshole, so my pleasure is tainted by guilt.

I move down to the pitchers. I look for Gooden and see that his ERA is 3.40, not bad, and he is 8 and 8, also not bad considering that the Mets haven't scored many runs this year. The thing that most thrills me about Gooden is his won-lost record, which coming into the year could compete with Whitey Ford's for the best of all time. And I remember hearing a friend from New York back in June of 1984 saying that the Mets had this young pitcher who was averaging a strike-out an inning and had an ERA under 2. I said I hadn't even noticed him in the papers. He said they were trying to keep it quiet to keep the pressure off him.

Finally, I notice the headlines about women's tennis; the only women's tennis player I care about is Jennifer Capriati. I became enamored of her when she was only thirteen and so much was expected of her. She's been very good but not great as a pro. I want her to fulfill her promise.

I put the paper down. In eight minutes I have gone on a whirlwind journey.

•　　•　　•　　•　　•

One irony strikes me as I look at the above. I compulsively identify with the glory of athletes and yet I have little identification with my role as a sports fan; in fact I find the image of myself as a sports fan painful to contemplate. I almost never talk about this stuff with anyone. I almost never watch sports with another person. I am energetically searching for something, and yet I don't believe in my search. I am mildly embarrassed by my involvement with sports. When I talk about it, I am defensive and self-justifying. What seems grounded in a grandiose search for identity shames me. Very rarely, around certain men, I enact the role of the sports fan just to get along and seem one of the guys. Sometimes, when I find myself in a bar with sports on television, I will play the role. But I feel sheepish, false, and uncomfortable doing so—a certain shame at trying to appear manly. I did this with my father, who died ten years ago. Maybe my fear of men motivates my connection to the sports page. I am both afraid of being different from other men and afraid of being like them; I want their acceptance yet fear and dislike them.

I don't *really* care about sports and yet I care deeply about *something* related to sports. A few years ago, I followed the Oakland A's every day. I wanted them to win and I rooted for them. They made it to the World Series. I watched the first two games. Then a dear old friend came to town, and I virtually ignored the rest of the games and didn't care when they lost.

What is going on?

One thing that is going on, a friend suggests, is that I have misinterpreted myself. I was raised in a family where sports were very important and where ideas and books were not. As I have grown older I possess a certain guilt and embarrassment about my residual attachment to sports. But, my friend suggests, my real guilt is about abandoning and betraying my younger self who loved playing sports, who developed math skills reading the sports page, and who got love and attention from his parents for his sports performances. I threw two no-hitters in Little League and was the first kid to hit a ball over our center field fence 240 feet away (my homer was estimated at 260 feet). I was an all-star halfback on the football team my Dad coached when I was twelve, ran for three touchdowns in one game, and was the only thirteen-year-old on the pony league baseball all-star team (consisting of thirteen- and fourteen-year-olds). I was All District in bas-

ketball in the tenth grade at fifteen and was offered a scholar-
ship to the Coast Guard Academy after my junior year. I
didn't play my senior year but became a hippie and an intellectual and a debater. So, maybe the real guilt is the betrayal
of who I was and what I passionately loved and who my parents loved me for being. They were not educated enough to
really appreciate the intellectual side of me and my mother
died when I was thirteen anyway. (I notice a young voice,
somewhat aspiring to be cute—and seeking nurturance—
has taken over here.)

•   •   •   •   •

Another irony. I am embarrassed by my banality as I read the
sports page, how much my experience resembles the experience of millions of other men who read the morning's sports
page that day. I notice that in pursuing one form of grandiose indulgence in the sports page I come up against another, more intellectual form of grandiosity. My sports consciousness pains me because of my involvement in another
grandiosity, an intellectual one, which is shamed by the un-
original, "inferior" sports grandiosity. I grew up in sports
grandiosity and somewhere in mid-adolescence, was taken
up by intellectual grandiosity. I have internalized two realms
in which to prove manhood, sports and ideas, and the two
are in conflict. (Of course, writing about sports intellectually
is one way to resolve this conflict.) I am embarrassed at basking in the reflected glory of athletes, but far less so in that of
intellectuals, an equally familiar process.

•   •   •   •   •

Let me return to the manhood-proving aspects of the sports page. The sports page is a balm to men's self-esteem, a realm in which one BIRGS. For many men it is the one place in the newspaper that guarantees pleasure. The athletes I identify with and wring glory from are successful at the tasks of proving manhood. They can endure stress and compete like real men. This is most obvious in football, in which enduring and inflicting physical pain is integral to the game, but it is equally true of baseball. Baseball, a superficially less macho game than football, is dramatized by sportscasters, writers, and to a lesser extent by players and fans, as a game offering situations in which one can endure the symbolic presence of the greatest stress of all—the threat of death. In baseball, putting someone out is killing and being put out is dying. Runners are *gunned down, mowed down, cut down, picked off like sitting ducks, caught dead* at the plate. Shortstops *rifle* the ball to first; the team tries a *suicide squeeze play.* As a corollary, not being put out is remaining safe— one hits *safely* or is *safe* at home. A batter fouls off the fourth pitch in a row and is *still alive at the plate, hanging on for dear life.*

All of these metaphors derive from a more basic one: intensely wanting and not getting is dying. One is *dying* to meet her, go to the bathroom, hear the news. I'll *die* if I don't ask you this, go to the game, see Paris in the spring. The suspense is *killing* me; I'm *scared to death.* It is as if the experience of intense desire is sufficiently overwhelming that one feels one will die if one has to endure the desire without satisfying it—as if high, prolonged, focused anxiety would destroy the self. One way boys and men prove their manhood is to successfully cope with such structured anxiety through games like baseball.

The death metaphors of baseball suggest that baseball is about a continual struggle with symbolic danger. The baseball itself can be seen as an agent of death; one wants to hit it as far away as possible so one can cheat death and trot leisurely, safely, through alien territory around the bases, and come home. The experience of being tagged out is a pristine, magical kind of death—the ball touches a runner on the basepaths and his energy dissipates in a primal, dreamlike experience.

In baseball one gets to confront and conquer the stress of fear in an ongoing way—one is afraid and safe and afraid and safe over and over again. And for young boys in American society it is an early experience of compulsive masculinity. Sports, or the excesses of sports, are, from one perspective, a form of indoctrination into group identification that prepares men to fight in the military; that is, to at least transiently anonymize an outgroup as part of a larger eventual preparation to hate and be willing to kill another larger outgroup. A teenage boy who learns to root for his high school football team and to hate his crosstown rivals is preparing to fight other countries. It serves very real ideological political and cultural purposes. But those purposes depend and ride upon other, deeper, psychic functions.

In holding a bat in one's hands and swinging powerfully a

boy identifies himself as a man and identifies with other boys who do the same—just as he first stood erect and urinated in a similar, perhaps prototypical, identification.[1]

This form of identification, the identification I engage in when reading the sports page, Nancy Chodorow has called *positional identification*.[2] It is what characterizes boys' identification with fathers—mediated identity achieved through mutual shared identification with gender ideals of masculinity. When I identify with sports figures and their statistics, I am identifying with a position and not a person.

Recall the argument from chapter 2. Predominantly mother-raised boys grow up identifying with a mostly absent father, often emotionally remote; girls identify with a mother who is more or less continuously present. Boys must make a wrenching shift in identification away from their mothers; a hole develops in boys' psyches that is filled with grandiose cultural models of masculinity that never successfully confer masculine identity. Masculinity becomes a lifelong achievement never quite brought off.

In this light the identifications of the sports page offer psychic relief to boys during a period of great gender confusion. The unassailable precision of baseball statistics brings moral clarity and integrity to the process. In hitting at least, the greater the number, the greater the manhood. My father, an army officer, was gone for one-and-a-half years of the first nine years of my life. He worked hard five days a week and half a day on Saturdays. His physical absence and psychic remoteness made positional identification a necessity.

I started on the sports page when I was five, looking at the pictures, and baseball cards soon became a source of magic. We bonded around the watching and playing of sports. I developed my attraction to the sports page when I was struggling to establish my maleness, and the habit just lingered on.

For those males short of self-esteem and struggling to achieve it, masculinity equals self-esteem. The pull of maternal identification, most present during distress, equals the loss of self-esteem. Compulsively identifying with sports figures who heroically achieve success in the face of distress offers one salve for self-esteem.

· · · · · ·

But still, what *is* it about those numbers: home runs, RBIs, runs scored, batting averages? Why do I thrill so at the thought of anybody knocking in 160 RBIs in a season or hitting fifty home runs? What is it about the numbers that have such a hold? Wherein lies their magic and awe? Major league players are walking numbers; their batting averages and number of home runs and RBIs and runs follow them around. What is the thrill of such extraordinary numbers? It is precision BIRGing. When I was in the seventh grade and played my first basketball game and scored eleven points, there was something magical about that number and my identification with it. As a child I remember the thrill of numbers on baseball cards and my awe when I came across great numbers; there is something behind this thrill that eludes explanation, some pristine source of childlike awe.

· · · · ·

What is the relation between the sports page, BIRGing, and sexism? The sports page crystallizes a problem for men that I alluded to in the last chapter: the mistaking of admiration for love. I think this has its roots in the act of shifting identification from mother to father and the attempt to substitute male glory for the safety one got from one's mother, and thereby disempower the mother. The hollowness of male glory is a dirty little secret men do not want to admit. It keeps men from intimacy with women and with themselves, and leads to excessive emotional demands on women. And it is difficult if not impossible to seek male glory, whether in actuality or through BIRGing, without seeking superiority to women.

Male sports also risk lapsing into sexism by viewing women as inferior because women cannot for the most part compete with men in sports. Finally, a point so obvious as to be subtle, the enormous space that male sports take up in American culture, much of which by some distributive right should belong to women, constitutes a pervasive form of sexism.

6

Homophobia

Straight men especially have a strange paranoia about feelings, and
they fear what they perceive in themselves and in gay men as weakness: femininity, softness, crying too easily. And you know, that's
their limitation that's coming out. What they twitch from in us is
what we have to nourish and make even stronger.

Paul Monette, in Mark Thompson's Gay Soul

Homophobia is entirely about extinguishing the feminine and
extinguishing the child. Because what are the two enemies of the
masculine myth—the woman and the child!

Andrew Harvey, in Mark Thompson's Gay Soul

GAY HATING

The record of straight men's behavior toward gays and lesbians has been, and largely remains, abominable. It ought to
be easy to see that straights have systematically abused and
oppressed gay people and continue to do so, but this perception eludes most straight men. Such a perception is intellectually obvious; the obstacles to its achievement lie outside
the realm of mere intellection.

We have no single word for the hatred of gays—this fact
alone reflects our unwillingness to acknowledge the prob-

lem. "Homophobia" psychologizes the problem; "hetero-sexism" addresses structural issues of oppression and the privileging of heterosexuals; but neither addresses the intensity of the hatred. Growing up in the deep South in the 1950s, the most powerful hatred I encountered was directed not at blacks but at gays. Though racism was rampant, it was partially balanced by a sense among some that racism was wrong; there were real black people around whose humanity was visible, and simple human decency could at times prevail. But gays were not visible and were thus available as repositories of the most horrendous projections.

I don't know at what age it started but by sixth grade this hatred was going full blaze:

"When you wake up in the morning do you have hair between your teeth?"

"No."

"You're a professional."

If you said yes, you were told you were an amateur. And epithets spewed out of boys' mouths: "Q-ball! Queerball! Queer!" And a little later, "Cocksucker!" or "That sucks!" It was rampant around boys my age until I was eighteen and left for college, where other perspectives began to prevail.

The insecurity of straight men about our heterosexuality/masculinity is, to judge from our behavior, enormous and even hysterical. As Jeffrey Weeks points out, heterosexuality is embroiled in a deep contradiction.[1] Heterosexuality is at once presented as the most natural thing in the world, and yet so many straight men behave as if it were perpetually fragile, and in danger of being undercut by any association with gays. How can something so supposedly "natural" be threatened by something so supposedly "unnatural"? Part of the answer lies in the fact that heterosexuality is equated with masculinity, which I have argued is, for many men, under perpetual psychic threat. The uncoupling of heterosexuality and masculinity would itself be a force against homophobia—if heterosexual desire and activity did not prove masculinity, homosexual desire and activity would not disprove it.

It is useful to be struck by—and not easy to be struck by—another contradiction: the existence of as many gay men as possible is, from the perspective of the mentality of sexual scarcity that afflicts so many straight men, in their objective, rational self-interest; and yet so few straight men welcome the existence of gays. We are so accustomed to the hostility of straights to gays that we rarely notice that straight men—especially adolescent and postadolescent straight men—compete, sometimes desperately, for the attention of women and benefit from the existence of men who offer no competition. This suggests the degree to which the hatred of gays is motivated by psychological needs. One can argue that racism and sexism are in the very narrowly conceived self-interest of those who propagate them, but it is harder to see this about homophobia.

Presumably, the fear of being raped by other men is an objective danger implicit in the very existence of gays, as Terry Kupers suggests.[2] Arguably, we should distinguish homophobia in straight men that focuses on the fear of being raped by strong macho gays, from homophobia that is threatened by gay effeminacy.[3] Straight men realize how hostile their own lust for women can be and fear being on the receiving end of that lust from men. Still, the sources of homophobia must be sought not in the objective self-interests of straights but in the realm of the psychological and irrational.

·   ·   ·   ·   ·

It is important to distinguish homophobia as an anxiety in straight men about their possible, or actual, homoerotic feelings and fantasies, from homophobia as the enacted oppression of gays by straights. The ability of straights to acknowledge and explore homophobia in the first sense is a step toward ending it in the second. Experiencing one's homophobia in the first sense is to be encouraged; enacting it in the second is to be condemned and its institutionalization, where possible, politically and legally remedied.[4] This distinction is important; if straight men are to become the allies of gay men they may have to confront their discomfort with their (real or, more likely, imagined) homoerotic sides. I take it that most straight men possess homophobic anxieties, whether consciously admitted or not; to simply label such feelings as "homophobia" and therefore "bad" closes off the possibilities of psychological and political exploration needed for straight men to engage in antihomophobic actions and to achieve self-knowledge. The more friendly straight men are with their homophobic anxieties, the more friendly they are likely to be toward gay men. Far too much

pro-gay writing conflates homophobic oppression with homophobic anxiety in straight men, and uselessly condemns
the latter.

I take it as true that, generally, men who oppress gays are
likely to be men who oppress women, and likely to be more
compulsively masculine; that homophobia and sexism have
in common difficulty empathizing with and treating as fully
human, people who have sex with men—gays and (most)
women. And that homophobia essentially is grounded in the
hatred of any appearance of what is regarded as "feminine"
in men. Straight men in part fear the feminine in men because they fear possible arousal, or the attempt at arousal, by
effeminate gay men.

Homophobia and sexism are thus best understood in relation to each other. Homophobic anxiety sometimes eats
away at straight men. It is in part the fear that something ar-
duously and painfully achieved, masculinity, will be forever
lost if one gives in to certain impulses. It is in part inexorably
tied to shame—the fear of being seen as gay by other men.
Many straight men so strongly conjoin sexual object choice
and achieved masculinity that they have great difficulty separating them.

PSYCHOANALYTIC SOURCES OF HOMOPHOBIA

I want to flesh out insights I hinted at in chapters 2 and 3 derived from the preoedipal scenario. Recall that predomi-

nantly mother-raised boys begin life more or less identified with their mothers and, at a certain point, must make a shift in identification to a remote father, and to grandiose stereotypes of masculinity. This shift is never quite successful; hence masculinity remains problematic throughout life.

Following the important work of gay psychoanalyst Richard Isay, I believe that we come into the world with biologically based impulsions to be sexually attracted to either the same or the opposite sex, or in varying degrees, both, and that social context and the social generally can powerfully, sometimes transiently, influence object choice. (I will not argue this point here.)[5] But the process of psychosexual development allows for complex motives for attraction or pseudoattraction, or lustless sexual fantasy, grounded in, among other things, processes of gender identification. There is a tendency to assume that sexual object choice as enacted in behavior, private sexual fantasy, felt gender identity, displayed gender identity, mode of sexual satisfaction, and biological sex will be in natural "alignment." That is, a biological male will act straight, have straight fantasies, feel internally like a "man" and act like one, and prefer conventional intercourse. But all of these characteristics can manifest in different forms and combinations. And sexual desire and fantasy can mean many things. Fantasies of engaging in sexual acts may not express sexual desire.

I want to distinguish among the following. First, there is lust toward one's own sex that is driven toward orgasm, something I take to be biologically impelled and a powerful source of fantasy. Such lust may be attached to any number of emotions. Second, there is an affectional consciousness toward members of one's own sex in which identification and attraction are difficult to separate. Third, there are fantasies of sexual activity with members of one's own sex that are not charged with lust and do not lead to orgasm. One's ability to relate to such distinctions will be constrained by one's experience. Lust centers around genital arousal and the desire to discharge in orgasm. An affectional consciousness is not driven by lust. And fantasies of erotic acts uncharged by lust are driven by psychological motivation usually related to processes of identification.

With these distinctions in mind, I want to explore three developmental moments that may motivate heterosexual men (men biologically impelled toward heterosexuality) toward forms of erotic or eroticized consciousness of men in ways that are likely to threaten manhood. All of them center around the concept of identification; one relates to the original identification with mother; a second relates to the process of shifting identification to father; and a third relates to the process of identifying with mother's models of masculinity.

These are meant only to be conceptually distinct; in life they may work together in a number of ways.

The first point has been expressed well by Michael Kimmel: "If the pre-oedipal boy identifies with mother, he *sees the world through his mother's eyes.* . . . He sees the father as his mother sees his father, with a combination of awe, wonder, terror, *and desire.* He simultaneously sees the father as he, the boy, would like to see him—as the object not of desire but of emulation."[6]

This presumes what I take to be true—that there exists a pre-oedipal stage of "safe" identification with the mother, where she is recognized as of different gender. This is arguably the strongest source of homophobia; it is not lust for the father so much as a mediated *erotic perception* of the father. The boy represses this erotic perception as he identifies with the father. The threat of regressing and identifying with his mother is a threat of loss of masculinity and loss of heterosexuality, or at least the awakening of an eroticized perception of his father. The two become psychically inseparable. Disidentifying with women and the "feminine" and disidentifying with gay men—twin sources of both sexism and homophobia—become necessary defenses.

Men become terrified of being seen as gay or feminine—a *fag, queer, wimp, sissy,* and so on. The animating emotion is shame. In shame we imagine we are being seen in a diminished way; we shrink and want to disappear or crawl into a hole and die; we curse our visibility. It is the eyes of others upon them that homophobic men fear, both of men perceiving them as less than masculine and gay men viewing them with lust.

The more tenuous the identification with father, the greater the fear of regression and identification with mother, and the stronger the need to resist. Obviously the more com-

fortable men are with their "feminine side" and their residual identification with mother, the less they need sexism and
homophobic oppression.

The second distinction and developmental moment is a little
more elusive. When the boy transfers identification to the father (and to grandiose stereotypes of masculinity) he also
transfers attraction; as he seeks to incorporate the father, to
become him, he also idealizes him and masculinity itself.
This idealized identification carries with it a form of attraction. In admiring and wanting to possess the muscles and
skill and swagger of men, one experiences a kind of attraction. Again, this is to be distinguished from lust.

The third distinction and developmental moment reca-
pitulates the first. As the boy grows up, the mother presents
a vision of men for him to identify with. In so doing she encourages the boy to identify with her image of a good man,
and her image of a good man is, assuming she is heterosexual, necessarily an eroticized one. One identifies with masculinity in part through mother's eyes. In sharing her vision
of the man she wants him to be, a boy shares her attraction.
In striving to identify with such men, boys perpetuate a certain erotic perception of them.

HOMOEROTIC FANTASY IN STRAIGHT MEN

We are very familiar with the idea that sex can be symbolized
in various fantasies and acts not themselves explicitly sexual.

It is also possible and arguably common for nonsexual feelings to be symbolized sexually. As Willard Gaylin points out we commonly use sexual language to express nonsexual feelings. When a man says "Fuck you!" to another man, or "I got screwed by my boss!" he is using the sexual to express the nonsexual.

It is possible to have lustless erotic fantasies, just as we lustlessly speak of "getting screwed" or say "Fuck you." Isay lucidly argues that among straight men homoerotic fantasies often express unconscious desires to be like women—from my perspective, to regress and identify with mother. Anal and oral fantasies toward men, fantasies with clear sexual content, can be experienced without lust attached to them or the desire to enact them, because they express desires to identify with women and not desires for sex with men. As Isay points out, "The unconscious at times expresses identification with the mother as fantasies of performing fellatio or being the receptive partner in anal sex."[7]

In Isay's experience, this is more common among straight men who "perceive their fathers as powerful, authoritarian, and frightening, and their mothers as submissive, dominated and demeaned by their husbands."[8] The fear of the father translates into a desire not to compete for mother's attention, not to be a man.

If homoerotic fantasy in straight men is typically motivated by a desire to identify with the mother, it is not surprising that homophobia and sexism are so deeply conjoined. Overcoming sexism means men empathizing with women—something men will be afraid to do if it means seeing men through women's eyes.

•   •   •   •   •

I want to briefly address two often conjoined assumptions regarding homophobia. The first is the assumption that if two straight men love or care deeply about each other, or enjoy hugging or being held by each other, they must be sublimating genital lust for each other, or be "latently homosexual." The second is the assumption that if men experience homophobic anxiety, or enact homophobic oppression, they must be repressing or struggling with homoerotic lust.

Both assumptions strike me as not only intellectual mystifications, but potentially injurious to straight men. If heterosexuality and homosexuality are both primarily genetically based, there is no reason to believe that straight men who care about each other possess homoerotic lust for each other. It may be understandably gratifying for gay or antihomophobic straight men and women to imagine the existence of such lust, but it is without clear foundation. Profeminist straight men sometimes, in reality or in imagination, try out a gay experience, seeking to find homoerotic lust within themselves simply because they believe it is supposed to be there. To establish an antihomophobic culture, straight men must be able to care for each other without needing to inspect themselves for evidence of lust.

If this analysis is correct, homophobic anxiety is driven

not by a lust for men, but by a terrifying *fear* of lust for men—a fear that behind one's affection for men is sexual desire. Behind this is a fear of losing masculinity—and behind this, ultimately, a fear of losing identity itself.

·   ·   ·   ·   ·

Finally, I want to observe some ways that homophobia constrains and harms straight men. Given the enormous suffering—largely unacknowledged by straights—that homophobia causes gays and lesbians, it may seem indulgent to go on about the ways it harms straight men. But in fact it does, and straight men largely don't know it. Or rather, have to be prodded to acknowledge it. If straights are to stop oppressing gays, it will help if they see it as in their self-interest.

The pains that straight men take not to appear gay or effeminate are substantial, unacknowledged, and self-destructive. Sociologist Michael Kimmel asks his students to list all the things that count as evidence that a man is gay. They mention, among other things, effeminate gaits or gestures, flamboyant or colorful dress, expressing affection toward other men, expressing psychological sensitivity about anything, expressing "vulnerable" emotions like sadness or grief, expressing strong aesthetic reactions, and engaging in traditionally feminine activities like cooking or sewing. By implication, all of these also serve as tacit injunctions that burden straight men and tell them what *not* to do. The acknowledgment of such a burden by straight men is an important antihomophobic step that needs to be taken.

Straight men choke themselves off from so many realms of expression in striving to prove manhood. It is hard for a straight man to live a full emotional life while straining to appear straight. Ridding the world of homophobic oppression will help free straights as well as gays.

7

Gay Sexism

Relatively little has been written by gay men about gay sexism; gays have their hands full resisting a gay-hating culture and coping with the tragedy of AIDS. In this chapter, I want to write from a distance as a straight man about gay sexism.[1] In doing so I do not mean to imply that most or all gay men are sexist; as I suggested in the previous chapter, I believe straight men have much of value to learn from gays and much to benefit from their liberation. I equally believe that straight men could learn a lot from the capacity of some gay men to empathize with women.

The first and most obvious thing to say about gay sexism is that gay men who are sexist are likely to be sexist because they are men and partake of the privileges that men partake of in this society. Whatever sexism exists in gay men derives from this more than anything else. But I want to ask two questions. Is there anything distinctive about the ways that gay men are sexist? And if there is, is there anything common to the personal and familial and social structures of gay experience that predispose gay men to these particular forms of sexism?

. . . . .

What seems to be distinctive about the sexism that can be found in gay men? My answer derives substantially, though not exclusively, from discussions with feminist women. I will focus on three things: (1) A certain willful, and tacitly hostile, ignoring of women; (2) a certain appropriation and mocking of, and competitiveness toward, the "feminine" and women's heteroerotic attractiveness; (3) a certain denigration of the "feminine" by gay men, as it is found in gay men. It is hard to separate this denigration from internalized homophobia.

As to the first type of gay sexism. A feminist friend was at a conference attended by many gay men. It was her observation that the gay men present, who were politically active, seemed to have no interest at all in the struggles of women that were being articulated. When she confronted them on this, they seemed to have no idea what she was talking about.

Another woman described a situation at her workplace where several gay men would totally ignore her in the halls and elevators, failing to adhere to even minimal standards of cordiality and civility.[2] It is only gay men who have treated her this particular way in any workplace. Other women coworkers had similar experiences.

Recently, a gay man I know, who has a Ph.D. in sociology and moves in progressive circles, did not know what PMS was; for someone in his social milieu not to know this can only be a willful achievement.

The second point refers in part to certain forms of drag, which some women experience as a put-down of women. Some gay men appear to appropriate and mock straight women's attractiveness, an act sometimes coupled with a seeming lack of interest in the lives of real women. My point is that drag *can* be sexist and is at times experienced as sexist by women (and men). The debate over when, how, and why drag is sexist is a complicated one that I will only briefly engage here. Men wearing women's clothes may encompass many things: gay men in drag; straight men transvestites seeking sexual pleasure (and perhaps paradoxically proving manhood);[3] joyous gender anarchy performed in any number of spirits; the transsexual longing of a biological male to be and be seen as, a woman; straight men resisting the oppressions of gender; and no doubt many other things as well. A variegated political content attends gay men in drag or gay men expressing a "feminine" persona. Drag can simultaneously subvert the gender order and support sexism. At its best, it may express hostility toward the gender system, may demonstrate the performed nature of all gender. It may reflect a certain awareness on the part of gay men of the rather arbitrary "performativity of gender" (grounded in years of gay men passing as straight), and may express affection for women. And yet, drag sometimes expresses and gratifies hostility toward women, both by those who perform it and by those who enjoy it.

A third type of gay sexism occurs when gay men refer to other gay men as feminine—as "she," "her," "queen," or by a woman's name—often with an element of derision present. Effeminate gay men are often denigrated. It is not clear whether (or when) this should be seen as internalized homophobia or sexism, but it speaks of an implicit hostility toward women. Homophobia and sexism are not always easily differentiated.

•   •   •   •   •

What might be structurally common to the experiences of gay men that might lead to the sexism described above? I will suggest four things. The first two are rather simple.

First, gay men are not attracted to women and (mostly) do not form primary economic and affectional bonds with them as mates. As such they lack one motivation straight men possess to relate to and understand women. This of course excludes them from certain forms of sexism straight men engage in—they do not (as far as I know) rape or sexually harass or batter women. But lacking such a motivation to relate to women makes it easier for gay men who do not like women to ignore them.

Gay men's lack of attraction and primary bonding to women is also a reason why gay men may be *less* sexist than straight men. They are less embroiled in the war between the sexes; they do not compete for control and resources in relationships with women as straight men do. And gay men are attracted to men and often critical of traditional forms of masculinity, which gives them a basis for identifying with and forming friendships with straight women.

Second, many women—straight women in particular—are homophobic and denigrating of gay men. This gives gay men good reason to feel angry toward some straight women; it does not legitimate the prejudgment of any particular woman, but it is an inevitable source of distrust.

The final two points require considerable elaboration. The first is psychoanalytic; the second, "socioanalytic"—it looks at the possible effects of social structures on the psyches of gay men.

Third, the psychoanalytic point is an extension of the wonderfully lucid and sensible work of gay psychoanalyst Richard Isay mentioned in Chapter 6. Isay believes, as I do, that for gay men sexual object choice is for the most part genetically determined.[4] Environment may influence how sexuality is expressed, but for the most part not object choice. He defines homosexuality in terms of the content of the sexual fantasies that impel a person toward sex with either men or women. If a man has predominant same-sex sexual fantasies, for Isay, he is homosexual.

Isay, working with some forty gay men in analysis or analytic therapy, has arrived at several clinical findings.[5] There is no evidence that the parenting of gay boys is more aberrant than the parenting of straights. Gay boys, somewhere between the ages of three and six, develop a sexual attraction toward their fathers; often, they adopt "feminine" mannerisms in identification with their mothers in an attempt to gain their fathers' attraction. Some, during adolescence, give up these "feminine" mannerisms.[6] While straight boys identify with their fathers and cultural stereotypes of masculinity in part as a way of seeking their mothers' attraction, gay boys lack this motivation and are likely to reject mainstream masculinity. They tend to be more sensitive and gentle, to cry more easily, to be more aesthetically oriented, and to reject aggressive masculine pursuits. Their fathers, consciously or unconsciously, sense that their gay sons are "different" and tend to withdraw from them, and may direct greater attention to other siblings. This withdrawal typically results in a lifelong wound for gay men, the denial or repression of which can be an inhibiting force in the expression of sexuality.[7]

The scene that Isay describes offers one potential source of gay sexism. If gay men are attracted to their fathers at a young age, they are of necessity in competition with their mothers and with women. As Isay puts it:

> Gay men may also be envious of and competitive with women, a feeling that they are often not aware of which originates in the rivalry with the mother for the father's attention. The description some gay men give of their mothers as being overbearing or binding, or as keeping them from their fathers, at times stems from anger at and envy of her closeness to the father.[8]

I said that drag often appears to appropriate and mock the heteroerotic attractiveness of women, and is experienced by some women as hostile and sexist. It appears to simultaneously denigrate and compete with women's attractiveness. One can find structural sources of such feelings in the childhood scenario Isay delineates, in which boys feel rivalry toward and envious of their mothers with whom they compete for father's attention.

Fourth, the socioanalytic point, which echoes the psychoanalytic one, relates to gay men's experience of their desired object's failure to be attracted to them. As a straight man, I try to imagine what it would be like to be gay. I can imagine life in one or another closet, the attraction to those with the same genitalia, the pain of being victimized by heterosexist oppression, the impersonation of false straight selves, the agony of coming out, alien and threatening (to me) oral and anal sexual practices, and the freedom to be affectionate toward other men.[9]

But I want to contemplate a particular social reality: for gay men 90+ percent of the people they are in principle attracted to—men—are by self-definition at least, attracted to women; and (something like) 90+ percent of the people who *are* in principle attracted to gay men are women, to whom gay men are not attracted.[10] (As a shorthand, I will refer to this as the Sexual Attraction Ratio, or SAR.) I take it that some such reality holds true in American society today, while acknowledging the reality of bisexuality and the imperfection of these categories, which are, here at least, roughly serviceable. I want to argue that the SAR must have a considerable, ponderable—if incommensurable—effect on the social construction of gay sexuality, gender, and gay sexism, and that it will echo and exacerbate the envy and competitiveness gay men may feel toward women as a result of the childhood scenario Isay describes. I will argue that the SAR will be of far greater importance in a homophobic world in which gays are driven into the closet than a world with no closet. Thus, homophobic oppression, both through its expression in women and its mediation through the SAR, can be seen as a cause of gay sexism.

Please note: I am not arguing that gay men prefer straight men to other gays. To the contrary, as I will explore later, I believe gays establish a psychic sexual economy, facilitated by the opening of the closet, by which they are much more able to recognize, and shape their attraction to, other gays.

An imperfect analogy may be useful for straight men. What would it be like if the SAR were reversed: if 90+ percent of those one was attracted to, women, were lesbians and 90+ percent of those one was not attracted to, men, were gay? How would this affect one's experience of gender and desire? What emotions and satisfactions might it animate? What defenses might it lead to? Take it a step farther and suppose one's attraction to women was totally closeted by a culture that ostracized one's sexuality, and the only public attraction to and from women one witnessed emanated from other women.[11]

Would this different SAR alone have important psychic

implications for straight men? It is impossible for me to imagine that it would not; and it is difficult to specify what they would be—my imagination begins to break down, in part because I have to imagine a different "I." It is important to imagine not simply how some constant "I" (the same "I" as "me" now) would feel if the world were this way, but who I would be, how I might be differently constructed. I would probably be angry at lesbian women in such a world, and I might be motivated to identify with women. If I wanted women to be attracted to me and the only attraction I saw was exchanged between women, I would have a motivation to act like women—and a resentment of women's attractiveness. I would receive a lot of rejection from lesbian women and a lot of unwanted attraction from gay men. I might find it gratifying to put down lesbian women by mocking them. It has been argued that gay and straight men have more in common sexually than either of them realize, that gender is a prime organizer of sexuality. I do not dispute this, but there is another side.

Consider the erotic flux of social life, something that for the most part occurs in the background, something almost always present but only occasionally represented. We regularly give and receive desire in all kinds of subtle ways. Gay men, particularly in a closeted world, give unrequited desire to men and receive unwanted desire from women as a (perhaps hidden) part of daily social experience. This will vary according to each man's place in society, his relation to the closet, his point in history and culture, and so on. And some gay men have painful crushes on straight men and receive unwanted crushes from straight women.

Consider further that part of the nature of sexual desire is to desire to be desired by the object of desire, the desire to be recognized and mirrored as a sexual being in the desiring response of the desired. If I am a gay man attracted to men attracted to women, does this motivate me to want to possess women's heteroerotic attractiveness?

Consider the experience of receiving unwanted desire from the object of desire of one's desired—gay men receiving desire from women. While some may find this flattering, some respond negatively, especially given that the source of unwanted desire—women—attract 90+ percent of those one is attracted to. Women's heteroerotic attractiveness has a dual meaning for gay men: it is simultaneously directed toward them and is unwanted, and it attracts many of those one is attracted to, who are not attracted to them.

I take it that the SAR will necessarily have psychic consequences for gay men, or at least I cannot imagine that it would have no consequences, especially in a homophobic world. The first evident consequence will be to replicate the early childhood scenario described earlier. Isay describes a scene in which gay boys are attracted to a father who is attracted to their mother and who withdraws from them. Gay men are in varying degrees likely to carry internal images of this conflict that can be touched off by the SAR, though I think the SAR in itself must be a powerful motivator of psychic gratifications.

And the feelings such a scene might animate? Presumably a general resentment and envy of attractive women. And specifically, it would be psychically gratifying to appropriate the heteroerotic attractiveness of women in an exaggerated mocking way, because:

1. To do so is to mock and satirize and satisfy resentment against sexy straight women for so often being the desired object of the object of one's desire. One simultaneously possesses women's attractiveness, while ridiculing it.
2. To do so is to satisfy a perhaps weaker desire to satisfy a perhaps weaker resentment toward women for the distress caused by their unwanted attraction to one.
3. To do so is to satisfy one's frustrated desire to arouse such men, that is, to satisfy one's desire to be the object of desire of the desired.
4. To do so is to satisfy the desire for revenge against straight men who arouse and frustrate one, by arousing and frustrating them in turn. And as straight homophobic men recognize that they are attracted to gay men impersonating women, homophobic panic may ensue. This is a way gay men can vengefully inflict homophobic pain and self-hate on homophobic straight men.

All of these satisfactions, and others, may be at work at once.

By the satisfactions of drag I refer to the satisfactions both of drag queens themselves and those gay men who enjoy them. Relatively few gay men practice drag, but it is celebrated in parts of gay culture. It is noteworthy that some famous feminine icons for gays—Mae West, Greta Garbo, Marlene Dietrich—typically possessed considerable sexual power over straight men while holding them in contempt.

I am also talking about a more general gratification in assuming womanliness, "feminine" personas, something Isay describes in young gay boys. Sexual desire and gender invite each other. Gender identity is invited by the response to one's desire, just as desire invites, creates, animates gender. Someone's desire is said to make one *feel like a woman* or (less often) *a man*. If gay men are attracted to men who give off sexual vibrations meant to make women feel like women, such vibrations may make gay men feel like women. Clark Gable's unabashed, dimpled gaze made women feel like women and made them want to look and seem like whatever they regarded as feminine. His attractiveness was directed to and, in a sense, generated womanliness. If one is attracted to straight men—or if in a closeted world there are few visible gay men—can such a desire also be generated? Playwright Harvey Fierstein has commented that he loved Clark Gable as Rhett Butler—"I mean if I was in love with Clark Gable, then I must be Vivien Leigh." [12] For a long time, sexual desire was supposed to inhere in men, and women were supposed to respond passively to this desire. In the past thirty years, we have seen a flowering of women's expressed desire. If men have been the containers of desire they have also been, to a degree, the definers of gender.

Presumably, to invoke a stereotype, part of the pleasure of being a gay hairdresser is to enhance, and identify with, the power of women's sexiness for men; likewise, the pleasure involved in being a gay fashion designer who designs women's clothes. I take it as objectively true that a disproportionate number of male hairdressers and fashion designers are gay.

•   •   •   •   •

There is a fairly simple reason why the SAR is likely to motivate sexism in gay men. The SAR is a force that drives gay men—partly in search of sexual partners—to live in certain urban "gay ghettos" apart from women. The less experience gay men have of women, the easier it will be to dismiss them.[13] (Of course homophobic oppression also drives gay men into gay enclaves.)

The SAR would be substantially less important if there were no closet. Consider the closeted world first. Outside highly sequestered subcultures, the only public display of sexual heat men can exhibit is toward women, and the only public sexual heat men can respond to is that exhibited by women. In such a world, gay men have women as their only models of sexual attraction *to* men, and women as their only models of objects of sexual attraction *for* men. Both as sexual subjects and objects, their only models are women.

Such a world will encourage gay men to adopt feminine gender displays for the simple reason that the public models of attraction directed at men all come from women, and the public models of desire coming from men all are directed toward women. Hence gay men will be motivated to identify with women's desire for men. I want to be desired by men; I only see men desiring women; I want to be womanly. I desire men; I see only women desiring men; I identify with women. I am simultaneously motivated to identify with women's sexual power over men and motivated to envy and resent women for possessing it. Such an SAR, combined with an omnipresent closet, will produce more sexism than a world with no closet.

Take the other pole, a world with no closet and no oppression of gays by straights. In such a world, there would be many public models of attraction of men to men, and men from men, for gay men to identify with. A psychic economy would come into play whereby attraction to straight men would be limited and less compelling. Where public sexual heat is freely displayed between men, attraction to straight men will be less important and the feelings of resentment, envy, and jealousy toward straight women's sexiness will be limited. One would expect less of a need for gay men to gratify angry feelings toward women, to adopt "effeminate" gestures or to do drag in a world with no closet. Of course, drag can also celebrate a certain joyous anarchic spirit toward gender, and the loss of the closet should be accompanied by the loss of gender as well.

A world without a closet is one in which gay men will be less sexist and less resentful of women. Of course, if straight women are no longer homophobic, that too provides a motive for gay men to feel less resentful of women, so it will be difficult to disentangle these effects. And if straight men no longer enact homophobic oppression, fathers will inflict fewer wounds on their gay sons and gay boys will feel less desperately competitive toward their mothers. A world without a closet is one in which more gay men will more easily show empathy toward women.

Epilogue

Sexism and the pains of manhood: the theme has repeated itself in these pages.

First, sexism is a pain for any man who seriously grapples with it. (Admittedly, not many do and many men have the luxury not to think about it.) It is painful to acknowledge one's own and other men's sexism; it is ugly and necessarily brings guilt and sadness. It depresses one's self-esteem and evokes anger toward men. And it's a pain in the colloquial sense: a nuisance, something that obstructs one's functioning, demands one's unwanted attention. One must deal with it and yet it would be *so* nice not to have to. Life is hard enough without having to worry about one's own or other men's sexism. So much energy can be expended: monitoring one's language; examining one's sexuality and the meaning of desires; inspecting fantasy; feeling guilty about the way one looks at women; feeling angry at women who believe they have figured one out because they see one's sexism; feeling disgusted with and ashamed of one's sex; feeling no longer identified with one's sex; feeling sick of being presumed guilty because one is a man; trying hard to treat women with respect and being accused of false gallantry; feeling confused about what it means to "respect" women; exploring one's feelings about sexism and masculinity and being accused of indulgence—and never knowing when "indulgence" will yield insight; wanting to be fair to both yourself and women and yet being presented with conflicting models of fairness so one never quite knows what is fair—and on and on until you no longer have the energy for all this. For these reasons alone, it would be very nice if sexism didn't exist.

Second, the pains taken to prove manhood drive one into sexism; they disable men from nurturing themselves through the refreshment of grief and from nurturing each other; they drive men to expect women to take unreasonable care of men. Men's pain will never be healed without a confrontation with sexism—men cannot be simultaneously fulfilled and sexist.

Third, the hundreds of invitations that every boy receives to become sexist is itself a violation of his humanity and presents a painful bind. This is no mere sentiment. To be esteemed by peers, boys must put down girls. Boys may face either the loss of social esteem from the disapproval of other males, or a covert and mystified injury to "personal" self-esteem through participating in sexism. (This is a lifelong problem for pro-feminist men.) Sexism derives, in part, from psychic corruption that enables men to distort and transmute their pain into misdirected anger and aggression—and self-glorification. The process of creating sexist identities in boys is one that simultaneously injures them and encourages the repression of pain. It is a process requiring our careful and exacting demystification.

Fourth, psychic pain, whatever its cause, is itself problematic for men in ways it is not problematic for women—gendered ways that undergird sexism. Pain often carries with it deep echoes of an ambivalent, unresolved longing for maternal nurturance, which if fulfilled could threaten one's identity as masculine. As I argued in chapters 2 and 3, enduring stress and distress is essential to proving manhood, and proving manhood always implicitly involves proving one's superiority to women.

Fifth, sexism cannot be adequately understood or grappled with without an understanding of some of its sources in men's suffering as men. This is a problematic but necessary formulation that can be easily used to justify sexism. Men's sexual violence and harassment of women are in part grounded in a psychically corrupt pain that enables men to see themselves as victimized by women's attractiveness.

And sixth, manhood—the deeply internalized injunction "to act like a man"—is a much greater pain than most men even begin to know. This is a truth men are slowly tracking down for themselves. The myriad ways in which men contort themselves to guarantee that they will be seen as men, and not as sissies or gay or just boys, wreak a psychic havoc that men are only beginning to articulate. Some of that psychic havoc gets acted out on women.

• • • • •

It is easy for those who contemplate the reality of sexism and violence against women—and the relative silence of decent men on the subject—to lose their compassion for men, to see them as some alien, monstrous other. And to see men who take no explicit stand against sexism as worthy of no respect.

On this topic, I am touched by, and draw counsel from, some remarks by Allan Creighton of the Oakland Men's Project, who has given well over a thousand antisexist workshops for teenagers.

> Just look at a group of teenagers hanging out behind your local high school. Just look at the way the guys are standing, the way they punch each other, the way they look at their feet, the way they check out the women as they pass by. It angers me to see what they already know about the brutalization process, about feeling afraid of each other, about feeling ridiculous about being men, feeling way behind and needing to catch up. I look at how they relate to each other, the jokes, the loud voices, how they're dying to get close to each other and can't get close to each other, and don't get close to each other.
>
> Now, teenage boys, especially older teenage boys, are already pressuring or pushing girls into sex, trashing them, harassing them, and hitting them, and from one perspective, they're the enemy. I want to say: they're not the enemy, they're just boys. They're trying to play the

part of men and they feel foolish and ridiculous, and
they look like they know they're ridiculous. They're not
the enemy; they've been turned into the enemy.

I sometimes want men to just hug these boys—they're
only boys. And I want to go in there and say, "Stop it!
Stop it! We're going to start over. Human Being 101.
We're going to start over at the beginning, zero to
eighteen, how you got here and what you really want
to do." [1]

· · · · ·

Straight men, more than we can admit, crave love. But the
love of women arouses fear of maternal engulfment and
threatens our manhood; and the love of men arouses homophobia and threatens our manhood. And so many men confuse love with admiration and, after desperately seeking and
even gaining the latter, come up bewilderingly short. I do
not know if it is at all practical to follow John Stoltenberg in
calling for an end to manhood, but I for one do not want a
truer masculinity, or a deeper masculinity, or a more secure
masculinity, or even a nonsexist masculinity, but rather,
none at all. [2]

R. D. Laing quotes a passage from Anna Freud in which a
little boy sits on a series of chairs, pretending. [3] In one chair
he is an explorer sailing up the Amazon, in another he is a
lion roaring and frightening his nurse, and in a third he is a
captain steering up the sea. Finally, in a child's high chair, he
tries to pretend that he is himself, simply a little boy. In time,
he may come to think that whenever he acts as if he is not
simply a little boy, he is pretending not to be himself. After

coming to believe he is just a little boy, he becomes a big man stuffed with all the things big men tell little boys. Eventually he becomes an old man playing at being an old man. But then he may realize that it all had been a game where he played at being a little boy and a big man and now an old man.

Masculinity is one of many ways of learning so well to pretend to be who you think you are that you forget you are pretending. All social identities are potential tyrannies; masculinity is one of the more dangerous. It is easy to get lost there.

.   .   .   .   .

And what is the use of identity anyway? Before we are men or boys or old or young, we are ourselves, alone with ourselves, both wondrous and terrified, everyone and no one.

Appendix:
Thinking about Sexism

So far as I can tell, I first encountered the word "sexism" in early 1969 when I was eighteen and a freshman in college. The word gave off a strange accusatory anxiety; I saw it in some alternative leftist publication and thought it was, politically, too far out, but soon all the people I admired were using it, and I followed along. I was a naive New Leftist, tormented by unacknowledged fear and guilt; my head lost in a whirl of sputtering ideas that came at me from every direction. I knew I was against racism and I hated the war in Vietnam; the counterculture was my home. Over time, sexism became something I also opposed, but with little heart or insight. I began to hear women direct the word at me when I said the wrong thing. I learned quickly to say the right thing. Above all, I did not want to be (or be seen as) a male chauvinist pig.

Since then, I have worked to gain a clearer idea of what

sexism is. What follows is an attempt to make the concept of sexism a little sharper, a little clearer, and a little more visible in its applications.

* * * * *

In lieu of a definition let me simply say that all sexism involves human activity that hurts women *as women*. (I am aware that men as men are also harmed in various ways, but I regard it as politically imprudent to call that sexism.) Because we have one word for sexism—and because we tend to wrongly assume that concepts contain and express essences, and because perceptions of sexism are usually accompanied by indignation, and because anger tends to freeze and rigidify cognition—it is easy to become conceptually rigid in thinking about sexism; that is, to fix upon one perception or conception; to assume that there is some essence to sexism, some one *thing* that it *is;* and to vigilantly inspect reality for evidence of that thing. There are many ways to hurt women as women—through thought, speech, action, social structure, policy, architecture, and so on. I want to make some distinctions about sexism that are sometimes blurred to everyone's detriment in the charged discussions that so often surround the subject. All distinctions are motivated; mine are necessarily politically motivated and aspire to demystify potential confusions. Sexism is in the eye of the beholder; there are many beholders and many situations of sexism. Until some agreement is gained about prototypical cases of sexism, however, little will be done about it. The distinctions that follow are by no means exhaustive or necessarily original; in each case they are intended to reflect real life issues.[1] The first ten distinctions relate to the harms of sexism.

1. *Idealizing versus denigrating sexism.* This is most familiar in the forms of Madonna (idealizing) and whore (denigrating) sexism, to which I have given a separate category.

Denigrating sexism puts women down and is familiar enough to require little elaboration. Viewing women as incompetent (bad drivers) or sex objects (pieces of ass) or weak (the fragile feminine) or children (the girls at the office) or stupid (a dumb broad) or in terms of their genitalia (cunts) are all familiar forms of denigrating sexism.

Idealizing sexism exalts women and is politically difficult because it is not always clear when the idealization of women inspires, and when it serves to injure, women. It can do both simultaneously.

In some cases the harm is clear. Adrienne Rich describes reading manuals as she prepared for and entered into motherhood in the early 1950s: "That calm, sure, unambivalent woman who moved through the pages of the manuals seemed as unlike me as an astronaut."[2] Rich was confronted with an image of psychic competence and equanimity that caused her guilt and confusion and feelings of inadequacy. Portraying women as more self-assured or in control than any woman could reasonably be is a form of sexist idealization, especially when the portrayal imposes an implicit expectation on women. Idealizations are probably most dangerous when they are presented as unexamined (and unexaminable) norms.

There is sometimes a danger that in opposing one dimension of sexism one will inadvertently support another. This is clearest in our next distinction.

1A. *Madonna versus whore sexism.* This is the most common distinction made about sexism. Madonna and whore sexism morally categorize women primarily in terms of nurturance and sexual accessibility; the Madonna is nurturing and sexually pure, the whore is sexually available and free of nurturing. While these are familiar categories, they are often referred to only implicitly. As I discussed in chapter 3, the feminist antipornography movement opposed pornography because it degrades women, that is, out of opposition to whore sexism; some right wingers have opposed pornography because it degrades *femininity,* itself a Madonna-sexist term that prescribes for women an identity that would deny women's sexuality. Feminists may oppose pornography's whore sexism; right wingers may oppose pornography out of support for Madonna sexism. These can look superficially like the same thing. Still other feminists have explored the potential of pornography to militate against Madonna sexism and have, in effect, been accused of supporting whore sexism. Much confusion has resulted from failures to keep these distinctions clear.

2. *Objectifying versus subjectifying sexism.* Objectifying sexism objectifies women's bodies; that is, it either ignores women's subjective experience or disrespects it through exploitation. It is probably rare for men to fully deny women's subjectivity. For instance, the man who looks at a woman

passing by on the street and says, "Nice tits," may be denying her any subjectivity, although it is more likely that he is experiencing her as possessing some specific subjectivity. Notice that if he says, "Nice tits, she's really hot!" he is clearly projecting a knowledge of her subjectivity, however skewed; he is blurring his desire for her with her desire. His sexism allows subjectivity in a narrow stereotypic fashion. But this is normally referred to as objectification because it reflects a lack of respect for her subjectivity and a willingness to use her sexually as an "object." (Again see chapter 3.)

We can distinguish this from subjectifying sexism in which men arrogate a knowledge of women as subjects, as centers of experience. Psychiatry has long been entrenched in such a stance. The 1975 *Textbook of Comprehensive Psychiatry*, still taught in medical schools into the 1980s, claimed that one girl in a million was likely to be a victim of incest. Social science research now places the figure at closer to one in six.[3] Following Freud, many psychiatrists dogmatically believed that if a woman said she had been sexually abused by her father, in all likelihood she was confusing fantasy with reality and expressing unconscious sexual desire for her father.

3. *Sexism under the guise of liberation versus sexism that is overtly injurious.* Violence against women is perhaps the most obvious example of overtly injurious sexism; other forms of such sexism are unequal pay for equal work and the exclusion of women from the professions. Sexism under the guise of liberation typically involves an authority claiming

possession of a privileged perspective or knowledge, who purveys this to women ostensibly to liberate them from suffering. Women internalize the perspective, typically as self-knowledge, and seek to liberate themselves through it and whatever practices attach to the self-knowledge. The practices are often attached to institutions that mediate the power of the authority claiming to have privileged knowledge. This articulation derives from Michel Foucault's notion of power/knowledge.[4] Such sexism can take many forms: the Catholic Church's construction of the feminine self; the writings of Marabel Morgan, which encourage an eroticized docility in women; the tradition in psychiatry of insisting that women will only find true fulfillment in motherhood and family; and therapy that encourages women to internalize and individualize crises in self-confidence upon entering the public work force, rather than understanding such crises structurally and politically. One can make a long list. Many versions of subjectifying sexism exist under the guise of liberation.

4. *Explicit sexist beliefs versus sexist background stances and practices.*[5] We can distinguish sexism that is a result of expressed and known beliefs about women, from sexism that results from background practices or stances directed toward women. A background practice is a taken-for-granted way of being in the world. For instance, we all intuitively know how far away to stand from each other in conversation. What "tells" us is the anxiety we experience when we stand too close or too far away. Much of the way sexism is

enacted is through practices and stances that are difficult to recognize and not consciously avowed. A male professor may honestly believe that women are as bright as men, but call on men more than women in the classroom; he may believe that women have much to teach him and yet interrupt women continually; he may consciously believe women are strong, and yet assume a tone of voice around them that identifies them as fragile. Changing beliefs does not always change practices, and, as is often pointed out, those with the "correct" express beliefs may be more sexist in their practices than those with "incorrect" beliefs.

5. *Sexism as personal prejudice versus institutional sexism.*[6] We can distinguish sexism that is "caused" by and expressed through psychological prejudice within individuals (like the sexism of an executive who believes women are incompetent and actively prevents their promotion) from sexism that exists in the functioning of institutions as a whole, perhaps as a result of their having been initially formed and organized by and for men. Take the example of a corporation. The organization of time and space, the way work is done, models of competence, notions of appropriate interaction, and conceptions of merit, pay, and appropriate vacation can all make work particularly difficult for women, without any particular man acting sexist toward any particular woman. It is now illegal to discriminate against women in the workplace. But many jobs were initially formed with the tacit assumption that employees are men with wives at home to take care of the children.

6. *Descriptive sexism versus prescriptive sexism.* Descriptive sexism relates to the misperception of who women are due to the distorting effects of stereotypes, norms, and expectations. Descriptive sexism results in the failure to perceive qualities in women that go against stereotype. For instance, the chair of an academic department refused a woman professor a pay increase because she had recently had a child and he believed she was not in a position to do much publishing. Although it was true that she had just had a child, she had also published a lot. The chair was imposing a stereotype on her of the harried mother and failed to take note of her publications—information that went against his stereotype.

Prescriptive sexism punishes women who do not live up to stereotypes. A woman at a prestigious accounting firm was refused promotion to being partner, despite high achievement, because she did not act "feminine" enough. She was told that if she assumed a more feminine manner and dress she would be promoted. Her employers accurately perceived her behavior as going against stereotypes of femininity and punished her for this.

7. *Sexist content of representations versus potential sexist perception of representations.*[7] We can distinguish inherently sexist representations from representations that can (and will) be related to in a sexist way, even though the context of their presentation may not particularly encourage sexism. Arguably, any image of a woman can be related to in a sexist way by some men. But some images are inherently sexist be-

cause of their content. Some feminists object to an image because they see it as being related to in a sexist way, while others may not because they see an intrinsically harmless image. The failure to grasp and clarify this distinction has resulted in serious miscommunication between the sexes.

8. *Sexist content of representations versus sexist framing of representations.* Some images are sexist not because of sexist content but because of where they are placed and how they are framed, that is, because of the use that is made of them. The framing of the image encourages the viewer to view them in a sexist fashion. In principle, any image of a girl or woman can be used in a sexist way. When *Playboy* places a photograph of their centerfold as an adolescent girl next to her nude picture, it is sexist; the photo in other contexts would not be, but the use made of it is sexist.

9. *Infantilizing sexism versus maternalizing sexism.* This refers to the stance of the man being sexist. Infantilizing sexism views women condescendingly as children; maternalizing sexism views them (injuriously) as mothers. Men and women both need to nurture and be nurtured; to be taken care of as children and to take care of each other as children. But sexism often takes the form of expecting excessive nurturance from women and denying their competence as adults.

10. *Sexism by commission versus omission.* Sexism by commission actively hurts women. But something can be sexist, as is often pointed out, by ignoring women. Much tradi-

tional history has been written as if women were invisible; medical research on health problems common to both sexes tends to focus more on men.

11. *Characterological sexism versus situational sexism.* The first ten distinctions are about the *harms* of sexism; this distinction is about the *causes* of sexism in individual men. In chapter 3 I talked about the fundamental attribution error, which states that in making sense of other people's behavior we fail to take sufficient account of the effect of situations and tend to overstate the effect of character. I argued that the sexism of pornography was perhaps as much about the situation of masturbation as about men's ingrained attitudes toward women. A man can say or do something sexist because of characterological attitudes toward women or because he is responding to a situation. Consider a group of boys using sexist language. One boy may be putting down women because he possesses deeply ingrained characterological sexism; another may possess considerable empathy for women but is using sexist language in response to the situation—to gain the other boys' approval. Both acts are sexist, but they do not reflect the same truths about the perpetrator. Women sometimes complain that their mates are sensitive to their experience when they are alone, but lose that sensitivity when they are around their male friends—a situation in which their husbands act sexist.

12. *Sexism as a problem versus sexism as a mystery.*[8] This distinction derives from Gabriel Marcel and deals not with two *kinds* or *causes* of sexism, but two general ways of ap-

proaching sexism. A problem, for Marcel, is something we can objectify and separate from ourselves. We examine data objectively and publicly in ways that qualified observers can agree on. When we possess requisite information our curiosity is satisfied; the problem is solved. Sexism viewed as a problem might look at increases in women's income relative to men or statistics on violence against women. Such an approach addresses women's condition in ways that are measurable and with agreed upon methods that lead to agreed upon conclusions.

A mystery may initially look like an intractable problem. But in approaching mysteries, the distinction between subject and object breaks down; what is in me and what is separate from me cannot be clearly distinguished. One approaches a mystery as a presence to be engaged and related to with all one's being, and in ways that are not explicit and easily repeated. Men and women viewing sexism as a mystery will differ in their approach, but they will center on the concrete relations between them. Straight men might approach sexism through a contemplation of the nature of their sexual desire, of the shifts in their experience of women when they are aroused, of the assumptions that underlie unjust anger at women, and at the feelings that arise when they use sexist language. For men, sexism as mystery involves confronting one's experience of women, both through the lens of one's solipsism and through leaps of imagination and empathy. It might involve attempting to concretely imagine women's experience while simultaneously recognizing the

impossibility of this. Approaching sexism as a mystery necessarily involves actively confronting one's form of intelligibility vis-à-vis the "opposite" gender. Relating to sexism as a
mystery can involve reaching into the nonverbal. It potentially evokes both wonder and terror as it threatens one's assumptions about reality.

13. *Sexism that results from applying gendered attributes to
women versus sexism that applies gendered attributes to the
nonhuman.* This distinction, like the first ten, is about harms
done to women. We can be sexist by expecting women to be
"feminine" and punishing them when they are not. We can
also implicitly support sexist views of women by seeing and
labeling something (say a color or a flower) as "feminine" or
regarding the yielding, "yin" aspect of reality as feminine.
The point is that thinking of certain aspects of reality as feminine legitimates an association between biological sex with
gender, and such a link can only constrain women's freedom.
What is needed is the delegitimation of such associations. I
am aware that Jungian modes of thought and feminist spiri-
tuality both may speak about the "feminine" aspects of the
cosmos (or the soul) in a way that may intend to exalt
women, or at least do them no harm. But this subtly perpetu-
ates the expectation that women be feminine and men be
masculine. This also has negative effects on men, which
brings us to a distinction no longer within sexism, but between gender oppression and sexism itself.

14. *Sexism versus gender oppression.* This is not a distinction within sexism but between sexism and something

closely related to it. Gender oppression applies to men as well as women. One's biology—one's primary and secondary sex characteristics—is given a cultural meaning that constrains who one is, prescribing that one be culturally defined as a man or a woman. "Man" and "woman" are cultural, not biological terms, loaded with moral content and implicit expectations that shift over history and culture for reasons often unclear. As Gayle Rubin has observed, gender, rather than being an expression of nature, is a way of repressing what is natural to our being.[9] Men are expected to repress whatever is considered feminine and women to repress what is considered masculine. To suggest that any quality of human beings or the cosmos is "masculine" or "feminine" can only ultimately oppress both men and women.

I am aware of the danger in these discussions of speaking of men as oppressed by gender, but it is clear that gender injures men and diminishes their humanity. I am not saying that women oppress men but that the whole system of gender does and, in particular, that men oppress men as men. Men, taken as a whole, do not treat women very well, but they do not treat each other very well either.

Notes

Preface

1. Harrison Simms, conversation with author, May 1989.

2. Richard Wollheim, *The Thread of Life* (Cambridge: Harvard University Press, 1984), 187.

Chapter One

1. Susan Brownmiller, *Against Our Will: Men, Women and Rape* (New York: Simon and Schuster, 1975).

Chapter Two

1. Nancy Chodorow, "Gender, Relation, and Difference in Psychoanalytic Perspective," in *The Future of Difference,* ed. Hester Eisenstein and Alice Jardine (New Brunswick: Rutgers University Press, 1985), 15. Chodorow, in her later book *Femininities, Masculinities, Sexualities* (Lexington: The University of Kentucky Press, 1994), cautions against the somewhat monolithic accounts of gender formation that characterized her earlier work—and that I have used in this chapter. Here I describe one psychic pathway to

the gender formation of compulsive masculinity; I think we need to pursue a variety of intuitions without allowing any to close off other possibilities. And we need to retain a sensitivity to individual variation in gender formation.

2. Chodorow, "Gender," 13.

3. An abundance of established work offers psychoanalytic feminist perspectives on what I am calling compulsive masculinity. Among the most useful books are Chodorow, *The Reproduction of Mothering* (Berkeley: The University of California Press, 1978); Dorothy Dinnerstein, *The Mermaid and the Minotaur* (New York: Harper Colophon, 1976); Jessica Benjamin, *The Bonds of Love* (New York: Pantheon, 1985); Eli Sagan, *Freud, Women, and Morality* (New York: Basic Books, 1988); Lillian Rubin, *Intimate Strangers* (New York: Harper Colophon, 1984), which offers a vivid and concrete application and exploration of psychoanalytic feminist ideas; and Miriam M. Johnson, *Strong Mothers, Weak Wives* (Berkeley: University of California Press, 1988).

Among the best articles are Beatrice Whiting, Clyde Kluckhohn, and James Anthony, "The Function of Male Initiation Rites in Puberty," in *Readings in Social Psychology*, ed. Eleanor E. Maccoby, Theodore M. Newcomb, and Eugene L. Hartley (New York: Holt, 1958); Karen Horney, "The Dread of Women," in *Feminine Psychology* (New York, W. W. Norton, 1962); and Roy Schafer, "Men Who Struggle Against Sentimentality," in *The Psychology of Men*, ed. Gerald I. Fogel, Frederick M. Lane, and Robert S. Liebert (New York: Basic Books, 1986).

4. Norman Mailer, *Existential Errands* (New York: Signet, 1974), 43.

5. Tom Wolfe, *The Right Stuff* (New York: Bantam, 1980), 22.

6. Michael Kimmel, "The Cult of Masculinity: American Social Character and the Legacy of the Cowboy," in *Beyond Patriarchy*, ed. Michael Kaufman (Oxford: Oxford University Press, 1983). Also see Kimmel's lucid and rich *Manhood in America* (New York: The Free Press, 1995), which promises to establish manhood-proving as an independent force in American history.

7. Gordon Liddy, *Will* (New York: St. Martin's Press, 1980), 24.

8. The issue of how work, indeed the Weberian rationalization of modern society, is informed and motivated by manhood-proving motivations is one that awaits demystification. For instance, will the massive entry of women into medical school alter the masochistic structure of medical training? The degree to which training for the professions is modeled on military training no doubt relates to the general militarization of society. The moral logic of the warrior still can be found throughout the world of work. Christine L. Williams has produced two thoughtful empirical studies about work and gender: *Still a Man's World: Men Who Do "Women's" Work* (Berkeley: University of California Press, 1995), and *Gender Differences at Work: Women and Men in Nontraditional Occupations* (Berkeley: University of California Press, 1989).

9. The likelihood that one will have to go to war some day is no doubt a major, underdiscussed factor among the objective social forces constructing masculinity and sexism. If a sense that some-day they will have to fight and kill is drilled into men, if they have to be willing to risk death, to die as part of their gendered identity, then childhood becomes war preparedness and women become objects of protection and thus inferior.

10. See Glenn Gray, *The Warriors* (New York: Harper and Row, 1967).

11. This is as good a place as any to suggest a possible relation between compulsive masculinity and creativity. To wit, I am intrigued by a parallel between creating and conquering stress as a means of proving manhood, and creating and conquering stress as a part of the creative process in art. Sometimes in the creative process, an internalized dare is produced as one writes the first line of a poem (or puts the first daub of paint on canvas), and prepares for the second. Does compulsive masculinity make such creative processes more psychically congenial to boys and men? There is considerable evidence that boys are more risk-taking in their cognitive styles than girls. And if creating and conquering distress separates men from mothers, does the same process in art gratify a

need in men to emulate mothers by giving birth to something new? I owe this last observation to Jim Stockinger.

12. See Jeffrey Fracher and Michael Kimmel, "Hard Issues and Soft Spots: Counseling Men About Sexuality," in *Men's Lives,* ed. Michael Kimmel and Mike Messner (New York: Macmillan Publishing, 1989).

13. David Gilmore, *Manhood in the Making, Cultural Concepts of Masculinity* (New Haven: Yale University Press, 1990). This book offers a wealth of anthropological data and a competent summary of theoretical perspectives, but is insensitive to the effects of compulsive masculinity on women's lives.

14. Albert Camus, "Reflections on the Guillotine," in *Resistance, Rebellion, and Death,* trans. Justin O'Brien (New York: Random House, 1960), 133.

15. G. F. W. Hegel, *The Philosophy of Right,* trans. T. M. Knox (Oxford: Oxford University Press, 1968), 263–264.

16. This summary is adopted from Harry Christian's useful *The Making of Anti-sexist Men* (London: Routledge and Kegan Paul, 1994), 10–11.

17. It strikes me as a plausible hypothesis, awaiting social science confirmation, that in certain geographically circumscribed cultures, natural selection will favor certain types of personality that will influence certain types of gender arrangements.

18. Elizabeth Young-Bruehl's difficult and important book, *The Anatomy of Prejudices* (Cambridge: Harvard University Press, 1996), appeared just as this one was going to press. There was insufficient time to grapple fully with her many insights into sexism and homophobia.

19. Sigmund Freud, *Inhibitions, Symptoms and Anxiety,* the Standard Edition (New York: W. W. Norton, 1960).

20. The classic exploration of this theme is Dinnerstein, *The Mermaid and the Minotaur.*

21. Henry Roth, *Call It Sleep* (New York: Avon, 1962), 90. Part of what informs this scene in the book is David's "Jewishness," which is perceived as "unmasculine."

22. Young-Bruehl, *Anatomy of Prejudices,* 132.

23. Ernest Schachtel, *Metamorphosis* (New York: Basic Books, 1959), 284.

24. Clearly these rituals have multiple functions. They create social boundaries by age and gender; produce and maintain structures of authority based on boundary divisions; and naturalize those boundaries and authority structures. They provide a moral sanction that guides social action.

Michael Kimmel suggests (in conversation) that in some manhood initiations men attempt to produce a second birth and arrogate the authority of the mother.

25. Herbert Fingarette, *The Self in Transformation* (New York: Harper Torchbooks, 1965), 79. Martin Heidegger has argued that if one does not clutch at meaning and one stays with anxiety, one can perceive the necessary arbitrariness of the intelligibility that structures one's existence and of *any* intelligibility that ever could structure existence. This leads, he says, to a certain zest and energy. See Heidegger, *Being and Time* (New York: Harper and Row, 1962).

26. Arlie Hochschild, *The Managed Heart* (Berkeley: University of California Press, 1983), 24.

27. Henri Tajfel, et al., "Social Categorization and Intergroup Behavior," *European Journal of Social Psychology* 1 (1971): 149–178.

28. R. B. Cialdini, *Influence: Science and Practice* (Glenview: Scott Foresman, 1988), 55.

29. Sigmund Freud, *Group Psychology and the Analysis of the Ego,* the Standard Edition (New York: W. W. Norton, 1960).

30. Eli Sagan, *Freud, Women and Morality* (New York: Basic Books, 1988), 118.

Chapter Three

1. I originally got the distinction between the authorized and the stolen image from a conversation with Erving Goffman. I apply it somewhat differently in my *Men on Rape* (New York: St. Martin's Press, 1982), 23–29. I leave it to women to explore the ways in

which their visual experience of men parallels—or fails to parallel—men's visual experience of them.

2. Erving Goffman, *Relations in Public* (New York: Harper and Row, 1971), 46.

3. See George Lakoff and Mark Johnson, *Metaphors We Live By* (Chicago: University of Chicago Press, 1980) for a fascinating example of this kind of linguistic analysis.

4. The notion of popular culture as "psychoanalysis in reverse" apparently derives from critical theorist Leo Lowenthal. See T. W. Adorno, "Television and the Patterns of Mass Culture," in *Mass Culture: The Popular Arts in America,* eds. Bernard Rosenberg and David Manning White (New York: The Free Press, 1957), 480.

5. Beneke, *Men on Rape,* 59–60.

6. *Men's Health* (24 July 1987): 41–46.

7. Hochschild, *The Managed Heart,* 40.

8. But I hasten to add that a strong case has been made by Diana E. H. Russell that pornography increases the incidence of rape. See her *Against Pornography* (Berkeley: Russell Publications, 1993). Russell's rigorous arguments deserve far more attention than they have thus far received.

9. I am indebted to Melinda Vadas, "Could Pornography Subordinate Women?" *The Journal of Philosophy* 84, no. 11 (September 1987), for stimulating me to think along these lines.

10. Susan Griffin, *Pornography and Silence* (New York: Harper and Row, 1981), 36.

11. Laura Lederer and Diana Russell, "Questions We Get Asked Most Often," in *Take Back the Night,* ed. Laura Lederer (New York: William Morrow, 1980), 36. It seems to me that in thinking of sexist objectification as the viewing of women as objects without consciousness, feminists have been bewitched by language in classic Wittgensteinian fashion.

12. John Berger, *Ways of Seeing* (Baltimore: Penguin, 1972), 54.

13. *Playboy's Women of the World* (Chicago: Playboy Press, 1985).

14. Sharon S. Brehm and Saul M. Kassin, *Social Psychology* (Boston: Houghton Mifflin Company, 1993), 113–120, or virtually any recent social psychology text. What I find extraordinary about the fundamental attribution error is the finding that, generally, people first automatically assume that behavior reflects character; only secondarily, and with some reflective labor, are we able to see the behavior of others as a response to a situation. It appears that people who vigilantly scrutinize others, attempting to "see into their souls," are more likely to commit the error, and may be *less* perceptive. This rings painfully true to my experience. Part of the process of maturing seems to involve learning to recognize the effect of situation upon behavior.

15. John Stoltenberg, *Refusing to be a Man* (Portland: Breitenbush Books, 1989), 121.

16. Brehm and Kassin, *Social Psychology*, 168.

17. Ibid., 169.

18. Chodorow, *Reproduction of Mothering*, and Dinnerstein, *Mermaid and the Minotaur*.

19. Marabel Morgan, *Total Joy* (Old Tappan, N.J.: Revell, 1976).

20. Michael Kimmel, ed., "'Insult' or 'Injury': Sex, Pornography, and Sexism," in *Men Confront Pornography* (New York: Crown Publishers, 1990), 306.

21. Harry Brod, "Eros Thanatized: Pornography and Male Sexuality," in *Men Confront Pornography*, ed. Michael Kimmel (New York: Crown Publishers, 1990), 192.

22. Sagan, *Freud, Women and Morality*, 45.

23. Lynne Segal, *Straight Sex* (Berkeley: University of California Press, 1994), 317.

Chapter Four

1. Stephen Goldbart and David Wallin, *Mapping the Terrain of the Heart* (Reading: Addison Wesley, 1994), 203. This book offers a lucid map of the mystifying psychic terrain of romantic love.

Chapter Five

1. See Phyllis Tyson, "A Developmental Line of Gender Identity, Gender Role and Choice of Love Object," *Journal of the American Psychoanalytic Association* 30 (1982): 61–86.

2. Chodorow, "Gender," 13.

Chapter Six

1. Jeffrey Weeks, *Sexuality and Its Discontents: Meanings, Myths and Modern Sexuality* (London: Routledge and Kegan Paul, 1985.)

2. Terry Kupers, *Revisioning Masculinity* (New York: Guilford Press, 1993), chapter 3.

3. Here I draw upon Young-Bruehl's typology of homophobias in *The Anatomy of Prejudices.* According to her, "Researchers using questionnaires and interviews have developed a profile of the homophobic person. He or she is authoritarian, status conscious, intolerant of ambiguity, and both cognitively and sexually rigid. . . . Those who are least homophobic support equality between the sexes" (152). The research suggests that the homophobe is a sexist and the nonhomophobe is an antisexist.

4. We could start by instituting strong antidiscrimination laws and legalizing gay marriage.

5. Daryl Bem recently offered a fascinating theory of the sources of sexual orientation, meant to apply to everyone, that he summarizes in the phrase "exotic becomes erotic." Bem argues that biology, in the form of genes and prenatal hormones, drives childhood temperament, which leads boys and girls to prefer to play with those of similar temperament. Most choose to play with those of the same gender, but some boys and girls prefer to play with those of the opposite gender. As a result of this, the same gender is experienced as alien and strange. We know that around those who are alien and strange, we experience autonomic arousal. When genital sexuality kicks in at adolescence, this autonomic arousal becomes sexualized, according to Bem—the exotic be-

comes erotic. Bem's argument is subtle and elaborate and worthy of much attention. It may be that some such mediation of biological termperament is at work in the development of sexual orientation, rather than a direct, inherited impulsion toward a given sexual object. See "Exotic Becomes Erotic: A Developmental Theory of Sexual Orientation," *Psychological Review* 103, no. 2 (1996): 320–335.

6. Michael Kimmel, "Masculinity as Homophobia: Fear, Shame, and Silence in the Construction of Gender Identity," in *Theorizing Masculinities,* ed. Harry Brod and Michael Kaufman (Thousand Oaks, California: Sage Publications, 1994), 130.

7. Richard A. Isay, *Being Homosexual* (New York: Avon Books, 1990), 77. Also, see Isay's fine book, *Becoming Gay* (New York: Pantheon Books, 1996), which contains a poignant account of his own evolution and coming out.

8. Isay, *Becoming Gay,* 77.

Chapter Seven

1. In this essay, I do something some may object to. I, a straight man, speculate—somewhat uneasily—about some possible social causes of gay sexism and displays of gender. I want to suggest, among other things, that the oppression of gays increases gay sexism in structural ways. But first I want to be clear: I regard all sexuality and gender as worth explaining or at least understanding and all sexism and heterosexism as urgently in need of explaining.

It may be that what intuitively strikes me as likely sources of gay sexism are simply wrong; that, as a straight man, an outsider, I am blind to gay experience and I project feelings and conflicts that do not exist in gays. Even if that is the case, I still think it is worth exploring my intuitions. First, my intuitions are ones that a straight person contemplating gay sexism is likely to have. If they are wrong, they need to be demystified and disposed of as part of a conversation between gays and straights. Second, it is useful to understand the sources of plausibility in the intuitions that derive from straight contemplation of gay experience. In that sense, what follows may be seen, or may turn out to be, an example of homophobia, or at least a form of straight blindness to gay experience. I hope my openness to this possibility is not disingenuous.

So I present the arguments in this chapter not simply as arguments per se, but as arguments-constructed-through-a-straight-man's-eyes. I have tried to present a little of the process and phenomenology that lead me to find them compelling.

2. The question can be legitimately raised to what extent some women gain self-esteem from the attentions and attractions of men and thus might be particularly angered by the lack of cordiality of gay men in the workplace, or elsewhere. This damage to self-esteem may result in hostility from women and may feed some women's homophobic attitudes toward gay men. However, in the examples here adduced I do not see that at work.

3. Psychoanalyst Robert Stoller argues from clinical experience that the arousal that transvestite men feel wearing women's clothes is a way of proving manhood—if they can remain real heterosexual men, attracted to women while dressed as women, they must truly be men. For a discussion of this, see Marjorie Garber, "Spare Parts: The Surgical Construction of Gender," in *Theorizing Feminism,* ed. Anne C. Herrmann and Abigail J. Stewart (Boulder: Westview Press, 1994).

4. It is likely that homosexuality is more genetically coded in gay men than lesbians, given the strong existence of political lesbianism—lesbianism motivated by an alliance with women and a rejection of patriarchy. In this section I rely heavily on the work of Isay, *Being Homosexual.*

5. I am of course aware of the intellectual vulnerability attendant upon any reliance on psychoanalytic "clinical findings." Supposed "clinical findings" have taught us much that is wrong and oppressive: that women who report childhood sexual abuse are expressing their own sexual fantasies; that gay men are gay because of overidentification with their mothers. So, why rely on Isay's findings? Ultimately, I can only say that they make good sense to me. If

one starts from the assumption that gay men are gay for genetic reasons (and straight men likewise), the rest falls into place.

6. Richard Isay has recently, through what he describes (in conversation) as a "different kind of listening" to his patients, come to believe that most gay men are constitutionally more effeminate and thus drawn to identify with their mothers. Genetic affinities may exist between some gay men and their mothers that predispose them toward "femininity" and further identification with their mothers. This is an intriguing observation that awaits further research. If this is the case, then this genetic affinity, more than competition for the father's attraction, is more likely to be driving gay men's feminine identification. I think one must remain particularly open to new research and theorizing on this matter.

7. The reader may wonder how the much discussed issue of "hypermasculine" gays fits into this discussion. It is not clear to me that such gay men are in any way unique regarding sexism. Anthropologist Gayle Rubin in a study of the gay leather culture observed (in conversation) that gay men involved in the leather scene struck her as no more or less sexist than other men.

8. Isay, *Being Homosexual,* 42.

9. Paul Monette's remarkable, relentlessly searching and honest book, *Becoming a Man: Half a Life Story* (New York: Harcourt Brace Jovanovich, 1992), more than anything else I have read, gives me a sense of what it is like growing up in at least one closet.

10. I am using the 90+ figure to stand in for a general social science finding that somewhat over 90 percent of the population, by self-report, is heterosexual. No one can be confident that people being surveyed on their sex lives are telling the truth, and there are always problems of definition, but at least by self-report the 90+ percent figure is the best we have. The most recent, and arguably most rigorous, study comes out of the University of Chicago. See Robert T. Michael, John H. Gagnon, Edward O. Laumann, and Gina Kolata, *Sex in America* (New York: Little, Brown and Company, 1994).

11. The disanalogies in this imagined world are strong here,

too. Those one is most attracted to, women, presumably in such a world would continue to have less power, whereas the straight men that gays are attracted to retain power.

12. Quoted in Michael Bronski, *Culture Clash* (Boston: South End Press, 1984), 96.

13. I am indebted to sociologist Joshua Gamson for this observation.

Epilogue

1. Allan Creighton, conversation with author, May 1989.

2. John Stoltenberg, *The End of Manhood* (New York: E. P. Dutton, 1993).

3. R. D. Laing, *Self and Others* (Baltimore: Penguin Books, 1961), 45–46.

Appendix

1. These distinctions are drawn eclectically from a variety of sources. In some cases they are in my experience original to me, though they no doubt are to be found elsewhere. I have footnoted the original sources I have been able to pin down.

2. Adrienne Rich, *Of Woman Born* (New York: W. W. Norton and Company, 1986), 35.

3. Alfred Freedman, Harold I. Kaplan, and Benjamin J. Sadock, eds., *Comprehensive Textbook of Psychiatry II* (Baltimore: The Williams and Williams Company, 1975).

4. Michel Foucault's notion of power/knowledge has spawned an industry of applications. For an application of this side of Foucault to Robert Bly and the mythopoetic men's movement, see my essay "Deep Masculinity as Social Control," in *The Politics of Manhood,* ed. Michael S. Kimmel (Philadelphia: Temple University Press, 1995), 151—163.

5. This is a key distinction in Martin Heidegger, *Being and*

Time, trans. John Macquarrie (New York: Harper and Row, 1962), the best explication of which is Hubert Dreyfus's *Being-in-the-World* (Cambridge: Massachusetts Institute of Technology Press, 1991). See also the section on the background in John Searle's *Intentionality* (Cambridge: Cambridge University Press, 1983).

6. This is a standard sociological distinction in discussions of racism. Bob Blauner has observed that blacks tend to view racism in terms of institutional racism, while whites view it in terms of personal prejudice. See his *Black Lives, White Lives* (Berkeley: University of California Press, 1989).

7. I first encountered this distinction in Rich Snowden's perceptive Men Against Sexist Violence slide show in June 1980.

8. Gabriel Marcel, *Creative Fidelity,* trans. Robert Rosthal (New York: Farrar, Straus, Giroux, 1964), 55.

9. Gayle Rubin, "The Traffic in Women: Notes on the Political Economy of Sex," first published in *Toward an Anthropology of Women,* ed. Rayna Reiter (New York: Monthly Review Press, 1975).

Index

lent consent, 19; effects on women's lives of, 27; fantasies of, 28; justification of, 25; and language, 29; as man's problem, 21; and men's attitudes toward women's attractiveness, 80–81

"Reflections on the Guillotine" (Camus), 45

Rich, Adrienne, 179, 202n. 2

Roethke, Theodore, 13, 128

Roth, Henry, 57, 194n. 21

Rubin, Gayle, 189, 201n. 7, 203n. 9

Russell, Diana, 87–88, 196n. 8

Sagan, Eli, 72, 111, 192n. 3, 195n. 30, 197n. 22

Schachtel, Ernest, 61, 195n. 23

Segal, Lynne, 111, 197n. 23

Self esteem, 68–69; grandiosity as flight from threats to, 51, 70, 13

Sex: pleasure, 101–110; relating, 101–110

Sexism, 177–89 passim; and "bitch," 30; characterological versus situational, 186; commission versus omission, 185–86; content versus framing, 185; content versus perception of content, 184–85; danger of justifying, xi; descriptive versus prescriptive, 184; as disaster for men, xii;

distinctions about, 178–79; empathy for, 1; ending in men's self interest, xii; explicit versus background, 182–83; fear of justifying, 1; first encountering word, 177; forces to end, xiii; in gay men, 7, 156–70; and gendered attributes applied to women versus non-human beings, 188; idealizing versus denigrating, 179; infantilizing versus maternalizing, 185; and language, 29, 30; as liberating versus injurious, 181–82; and longing for maternal safety, 60; Madonna, 7, 101–110, 111, 123, 179, 180; Madonna versus whore, 102–109, 180; men confronting, xiii; objectifying versus subjectifying, 180–81; and the pains of manhood, 171–75; prejudice versus institutional, 183; problem versus mystery, 186–88; rationalizing, 1; and sexual repression, 110–12; versus gender oppression, 188–89

Sexual Attraction Ratio (SAR) 4, 162–70; and the closet, 168–70

Sexual arousal: and loosening of boundaries, 97–99

TIMOTHY BENEKE is a
freelance writer and author of
Men on Rape.

Designer:	Barbara Jellow
Compositor:	G & S Typesetters
Text:	Minion
Display:	Arepo
Printer:	Haddon Craftsmen
Binder:	Haddon Craftsmen